Walking Labyrinths at Home: A Colorful Journey

(in the Sacred Colors Series)

Christopher L. Smith

Copyright © 2016 Christopher L. Smith

All rights reserved.

ISBN: 0-9985295-1-6
ISBN-13: 978-0-9985295-1-6

DEDICATION

This book is dedicated to those who will color it. It is my prayer that as you walk these labyrinths at home, you will be able to have time in reflection and prayer, connecting to God in the same way that people have from walking labyrinths throughout the ages in sacred spaces throughout the world.

This book, the second in a series, is also dedicated to those who have prompted me to explore my faith in ways that are outside the normal boxes. Special thanks is given to those who have pastorally guided me, including various ringing masters who helped me to find space for spiritual discipline as we walked through the campanology methods, the pastor of my home congregation (The Rev. Tom Wanner) who taught me that sometimes just walking with God is all that we can do and the chaplain during my first graduate degree (The Rev. Evelyn Newman) who taught me particular techniques to foster this.

CONTENTS

ACKNOWLEDGMENTS

Appreciation is given to those throughout the world who have constructed labyrinths as sacred spaces for people to walk. Additionally, credit is expressed to those who have photographed these spaces and provided details of their design, often placing these in the public domain anonymously. Particular appreciate is given to the photographer of the Cathedral of Notre-Dame in Chartes, France for offering their photograph of someone walking that labyrinth for others to use, include our use of the image for the cover.

INTRODUCTION

What is a labyrinth?

When you first look at a labyrinth, it is easy to think that you might be looking at a maze. It is laid out in a similar way in that there are a series of paths right next to each other going through a space. There are also generally entry and exit points, although in the case of a labyrinth the exit point may be the same as the entrance point, with the walker turning around once they reach the center of the labyrinth.

In the purest form, labyrinths consist of a single path that goes from the entrance to the exit (or more commonly the center which would require the walker to walk the same path forward and in reverse). The idea is that it is not a brain game or a puzzle that has to be solved, but rather just the creation of a path for the journey for the time that will be spent in the labyrinth. The examples contained in this book include two variations on this purest form. The first variation does not have just one path through the labyrinth but multiple paths, including the possibility of just going round and round a portion of the labyrinth before being ready to move on. This variation speaks to the fact that the path we are called to in life is not necessarily predetermined and that there are various ways that we can go on our life journey, but each of these paths leads us to the end. The second variation involves the existence of short dead ends that are off the main path. Unlike a maze where you may go quite a distance before realizing you have reached an inevitable dead end, you are able to see that they don't go anywhere but have the option to sojourn in the dead end before proceeding. This variation speaks to the fact that in life we do have to keep proceeding forward and instead of facing dead ends we embark on new portions of our journeys. Yet at the same time, there are times in our journeys where we are not ready to proceed on the path ahead of us and need to pull off in a layby or rest area to get ready to continue.

While labyrinths are most commonly seen in recent times in Christianity, they do predate their Christian use. In the great Gothic cathedrals, it was not unheard of to place a labyrinth on the floor in one of the great spaces to allow those who came to the cathedral to experience a mini-pilgrimage while they were there. Now, you will find labyrinths built into church spaces as well as temporary labyrinths (on big tarps or carpets) being used in these spaces for particular occasions. It is also possible to find labyrinths in outdoor spaces with the pattern embedded into the ground or constructed with maze like barriers such as walls or bushes. All of these designs for labyrinths require the person who has come to them to walk through them. In this book, you will have the opportunity to "walk" labyrinths using your pencil, crayon or pen.

Labyrinths traditionally were circular (or square) and maintained symmetry by regularly changing which ring they were in. When the labyrinth is designed in this fashion, there can be a regular rhythm to walking it. Modern labyrinths may take an overall shape of different geometric shapes (you will find many variants of this in this book) or even other shapes (there are some examples of these in the blocks that follow as well).

Modern labyrinths may also have some of the interior space blocked out to create a design, whereas historic labyrinths will fill the entire interior space with the path the walkers will follow.

Traditional walking of a labyrinth

Over time, many religious groups have talked about the importance of going on a pilgrimage. In fact some groups require its members to go on a pilgrimage at some point in their life and certain religious communities even have members participate in a pilgrimage to a place of importance to that community every year. These journeys are not just about the destination, but rather are also about the journey. The journey is to be used as part of the spiritual practice of the one who is on the pilgrimage. The pilgrim is to be changed spiritually by taking the time out to go on the journey. The problem is that a pilgrimage is often takes a lot in terms of time and expense. As a result, it can be difficult for a person to regularly go on a pilgrimage, if ever at all. In order to capture some of that experience, clerics in the cathedrals sought to offer a way for people to get some of the benefit of the pilgrimage journey for those who came to the cathedral and in a way that could be done closer to home and with a smaller investment of time. This is how the labyrinth arose as a tool to help the faithful in their spiritual disciplines.

Different spiritual directors will give different directions on how to get the most out of walking a labyrinth:

- At the very basic level, you can just walk through the labyrinth, walking in an intentional way.
- There are also simple things that you can be guided to do as you take your journey.
  - One thing you do is use a particular prayer of intention or relation (such as "Grant me hope" or "O God, you are all knowing and I need to trust you") that you say silently or out loud every time you take a step, sort of like a breath prayer.
  - Another alternative is to use formal prayers every time you turn. For example, someone who is Roman Catholic might chose to say a Hail Mary every time they turn right and an Our Father every time they turn left.
  - Another alternative that some spiritual directors will suggest is not something that is verbal, but rather to simply stop at every intersection and just listen for what God might be saying to you, pausing for thirty seconds or two minutes, or whatever is not too uncomfortable.
  - Another nonverbal alternative is to incorporate specific body movements into the traversal of the labyrinth, perhaps bowing, kneeling or even making oneself prone on the ground.
  - While there are many more alternatives, there is one more verbal alternative and that is to use the labyrinth as a way of exploring a particular spiritual topic. This could be done by reciting a verse of a psalm (or other Biblical passage) every few steps, prayerfully considering its implications in your life. Instead, some labyrinths place markers along the path to help you focus on specific things. One of the labyrinths in this book of this and markers are placed in the labyrinth for each of the twelve follows of Jesus.
- Of course, at the most complex level, a walker of a labyrinth could try and use all of these techniques. The problem with that is that the walker is likely to become so focused on the techniques that they are trying to do that they are likely to miss out on focusing on just being on the journey and the spiritual blessings that can come from that.

The labyrinth in Chartes is pointed to as the original (or one of them) and is regularly visited by thousands of pilgrims, from near and far. The instructions that they offer are simple and a good guide when choosing techniques that you will want to try. They simply say, "*Walk the path with your whole being.*" This simple direction is a powerful guide. Put your whole self into it for the time that you are walking. Put the whole of yourself into it whether you are walking it on your own, with others, or just with others around you elsewhere in the labyrinth. All of this is like life and life does require your whole being. Should you not offer the whole of yourself to God when you are trying to use a labyrinth to engage with God?

Walking a labyrinth at home

You may not have a labyrinth near you or you may not know where it is even if there is one. It is also possible that you are not physically able to walk a labyrinth. The good news is that you can use all of the techniques from the traditional walking of a labyrinth while you are moving a writing instrument over the labyrinth on a page.

There are also additional things that you can do if you chose to use colored writing instruments, with some alternatives working better if your medium allows blending of colors. Here are some alternatives for you to consider:

- Change the color that you are using at regular intervals, allowing the colors to reflect the different paces of your journey through the labyrinth.
- Change the color that you are using every time you come to an intersection or turn in the path.
- Use a specific color for when you are going in a particular direction (e.g. up and to the right, up and to the left, down and to the right, down and to the left) and change color when your journey begins to take you in a new direction.
- If there is an overlaid pattern on the labyrinth (at least one of the examples has one already drawn on it for you), change the colors as you journey so that you are coloring that larger pattern.
- Use color to reflect what is going on with you spiritually. Perhaps you would use different colors for when you are focused more on asking for something, simply speaking to God, waiting for answers and hearing from God.
- Use color to reflect how you are feeling. Perhaps you would use different colors for when you are calm, anxious, hopeful or other emotions.
- Use the shade of the color to reflect the speed you are moving through the labyrinth, perhaps using a dark red when you are "walking" real slowly for that portion and a light pink when your pace is more rapid.
- If your path will be one that returns along the same path, consider coloring in one side of the path on the way in and the other side of the path on the way out. Alternatively, just use basic colors and blend the colors of both paths together to leave the overall pattern colored with both primary and secondary colors.
- You can chose to color the space around the labyrinth before you walk it, after you walk it or even to leave it uncolored.

Each of these ways of coloring show you different things about your journey when you look back. The coloring will help you to understand some of the thoughts and insights you had while you were "walking". As you go through this book, it is suggested that you try different techniques for coloring just as you might try different spiritual directions. Doing so will help you to have different things to record in the journal/reflection pages that come at the end of each block of labyrinths. You can use those pages by writing on them as you go or by waiting until you have completed a block of labyrinths.

While you will not be physically walking through these labyrinths, walk them with your whole self. Make yourself vulnerable to what God has for you and engage in these spiritual practices.

FIRST BLOCK

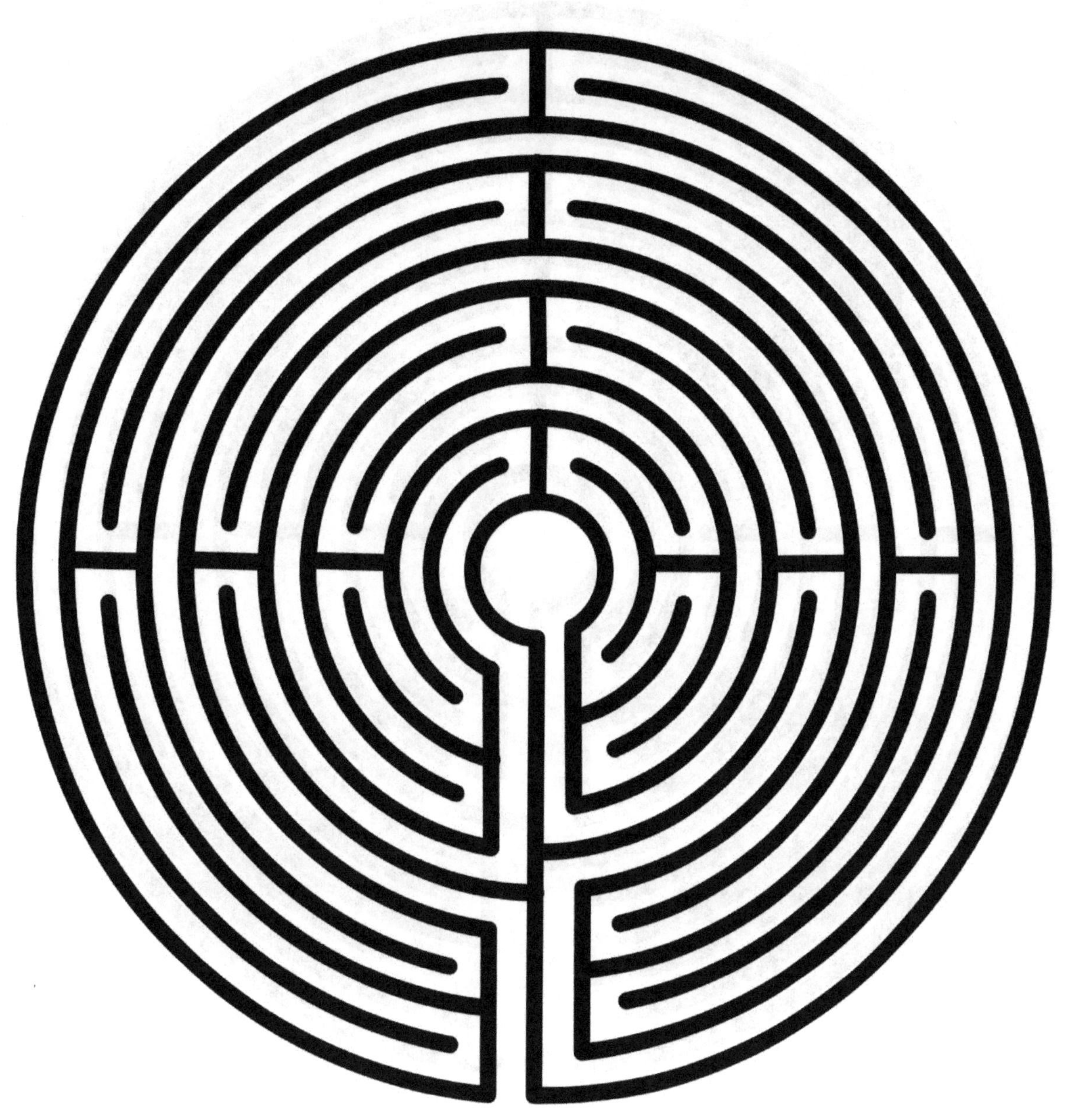

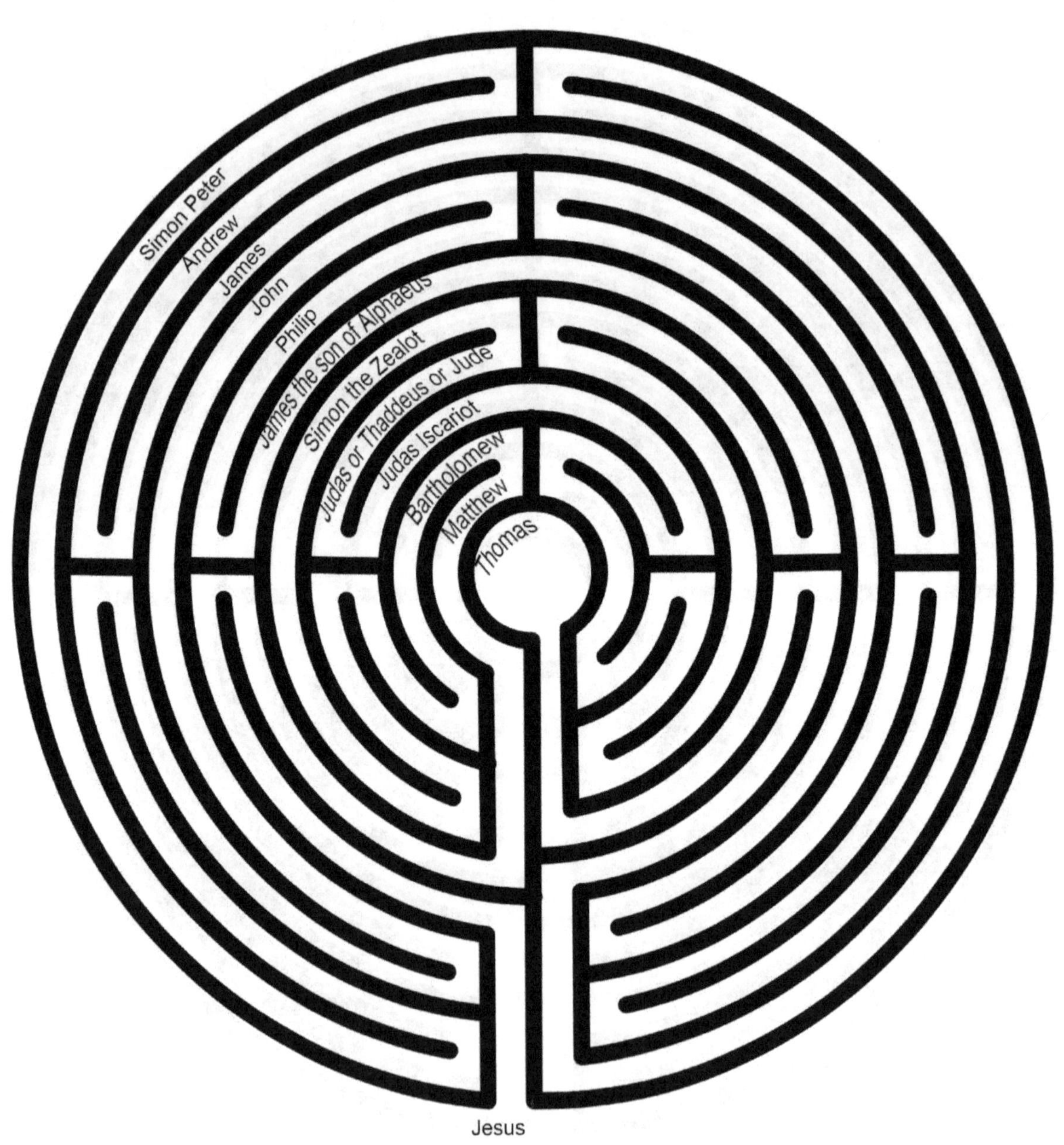
Simon Peter
Andrew
James
John
Philip
James the son of Alphaeus
Simon the Zealot
Judas or Thaddeus or Jude
Judas Iscariot
Bartholomew
Matthew
Thomas
Jesus

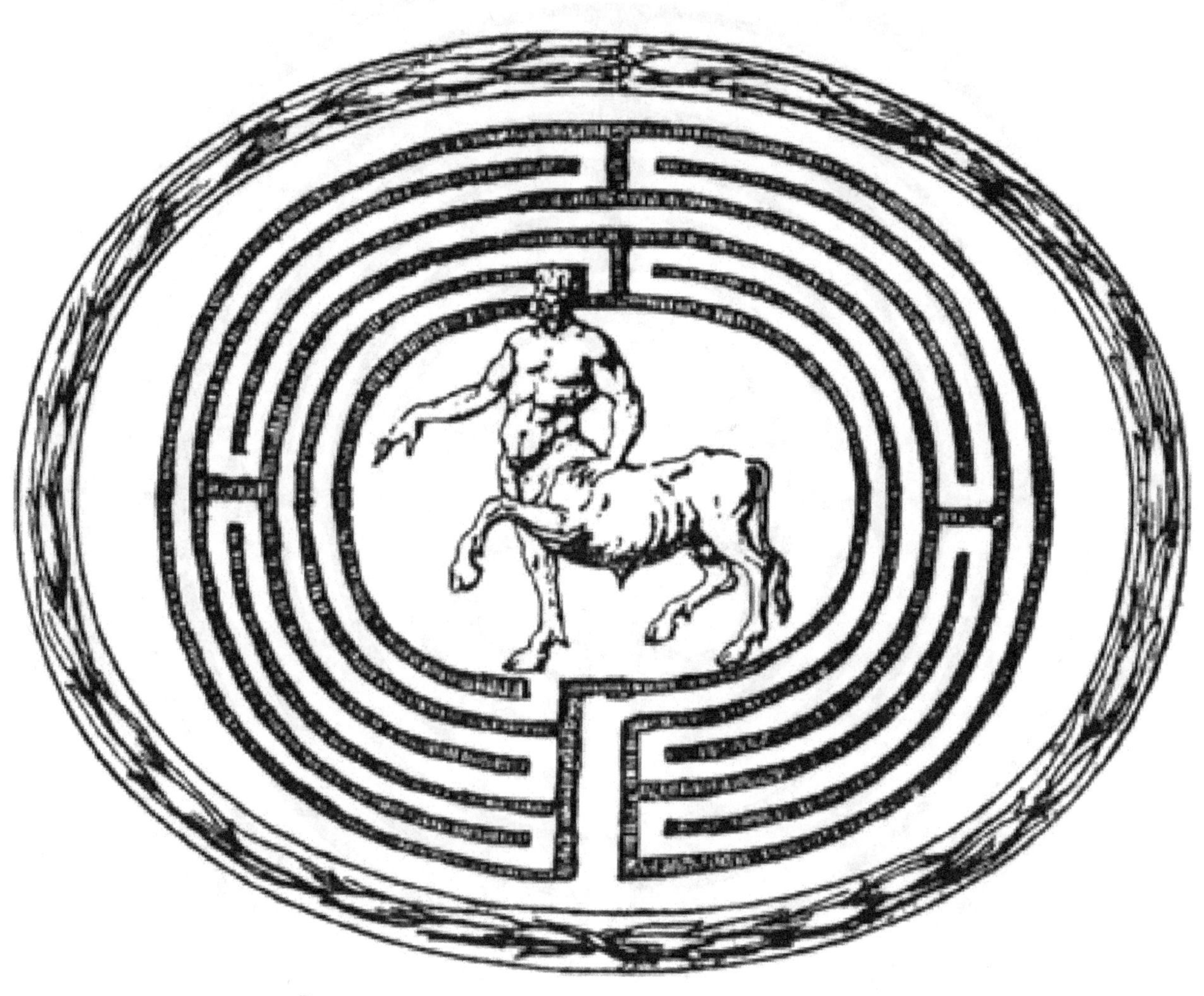

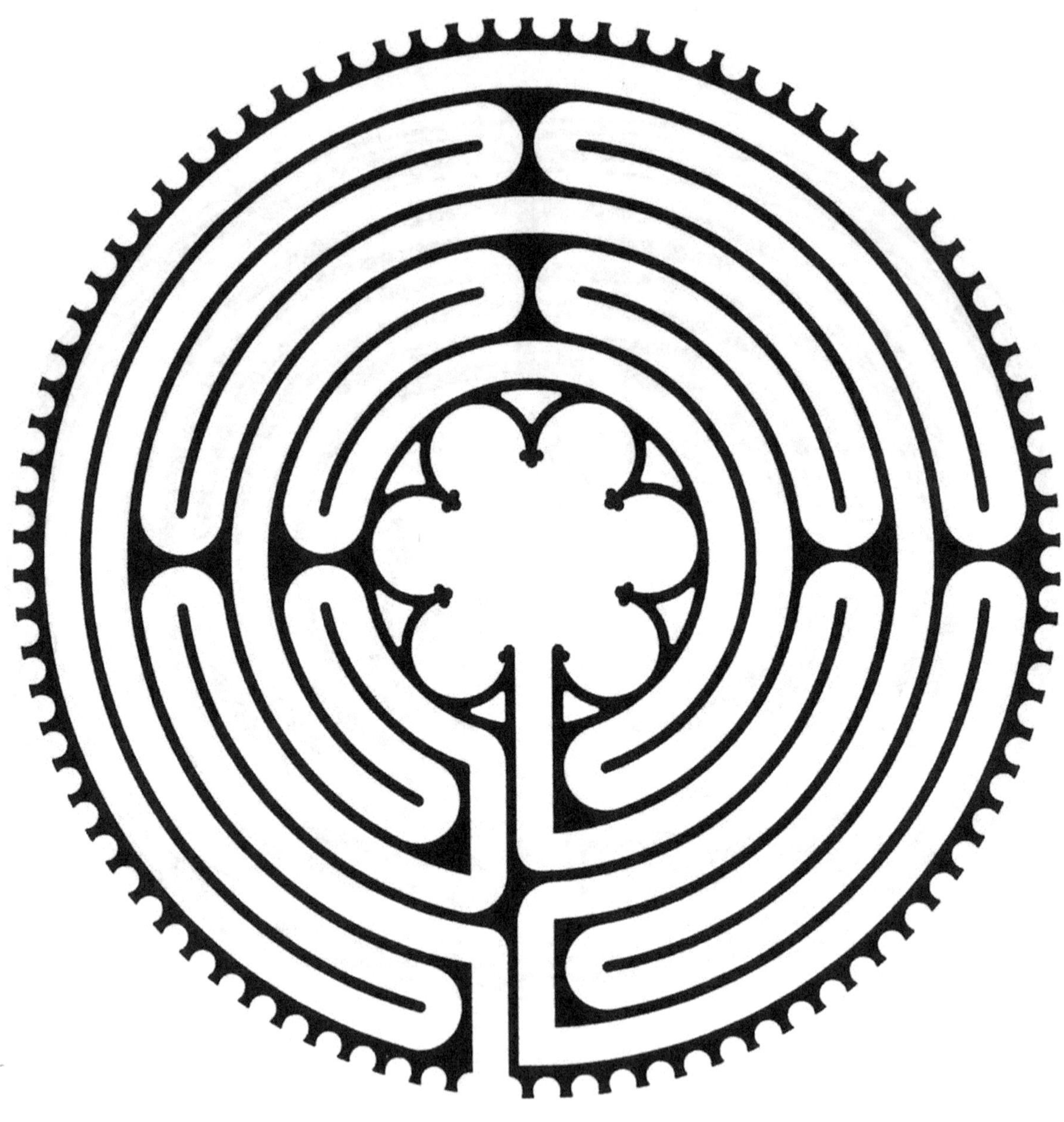

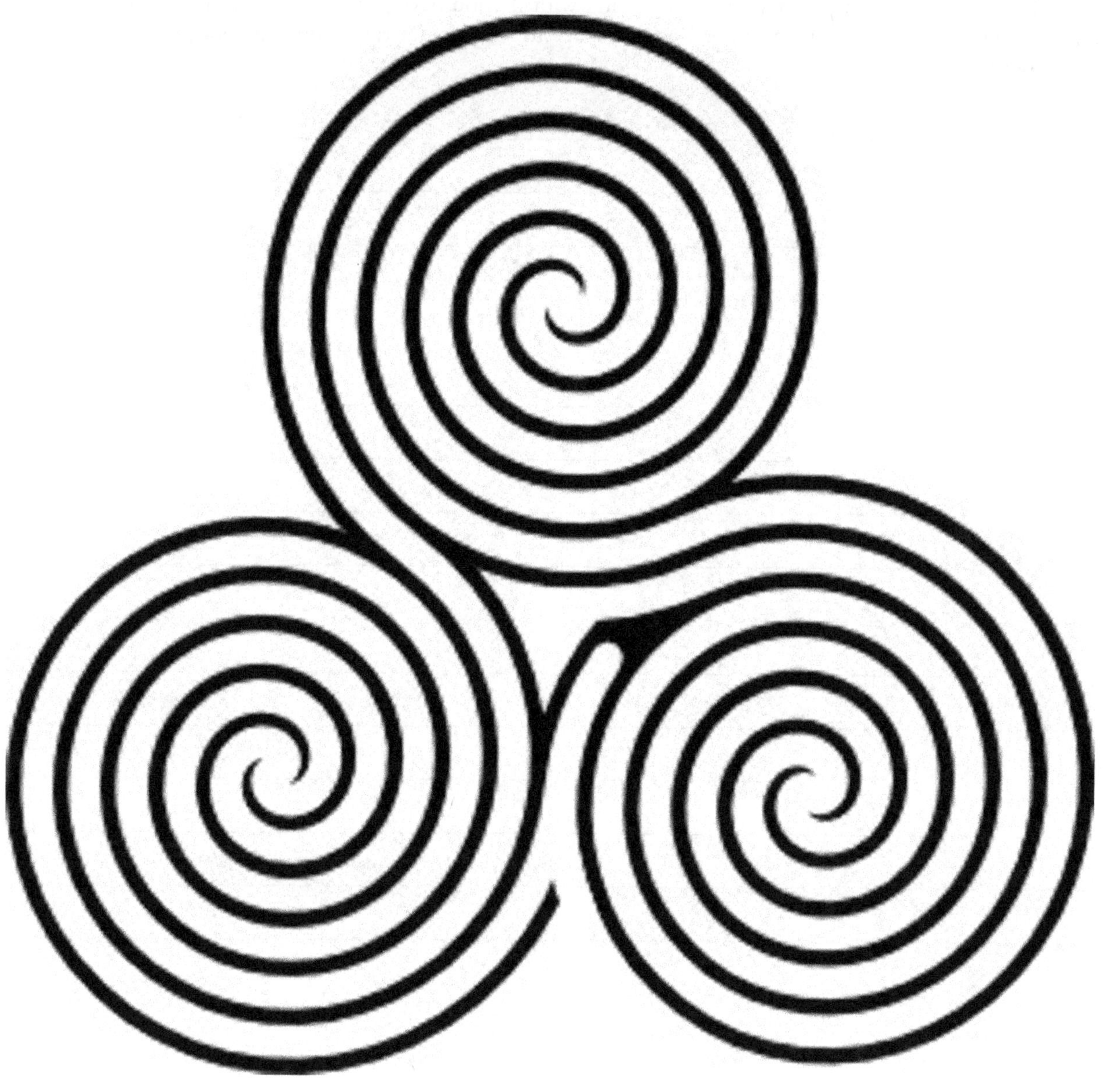

REFLECTIONS ON THIS BLOCK

Having walked the labyrinths in this block, what have you learned about your walk of faith? your relationship with God? ways in which you have difficulty being with the journey? parts of you that you hold back from fully engaging? lessons you are learning? Use this space to record your reflections on your journeys or arising from your journeys.

SECOND BLOCK

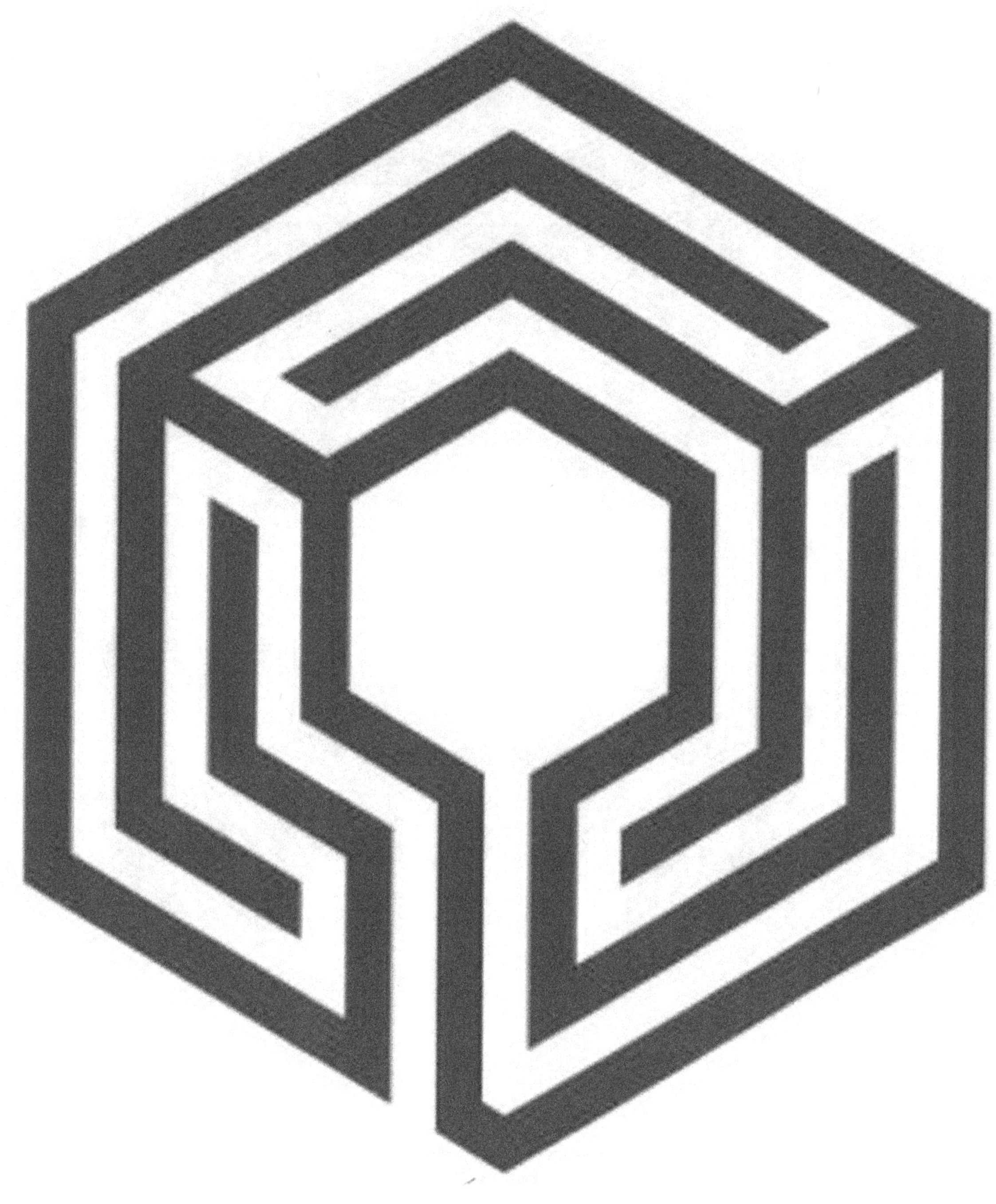

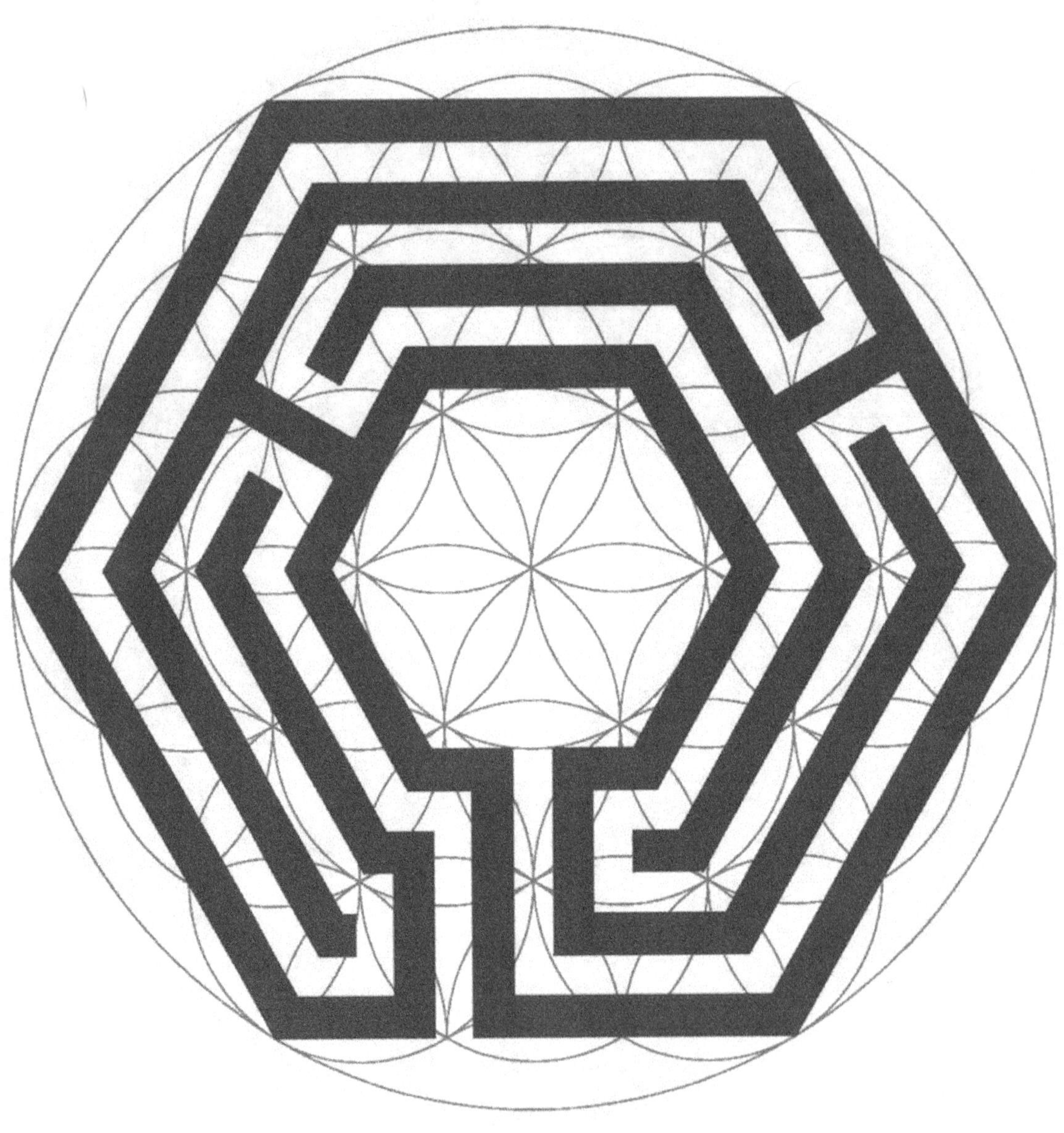

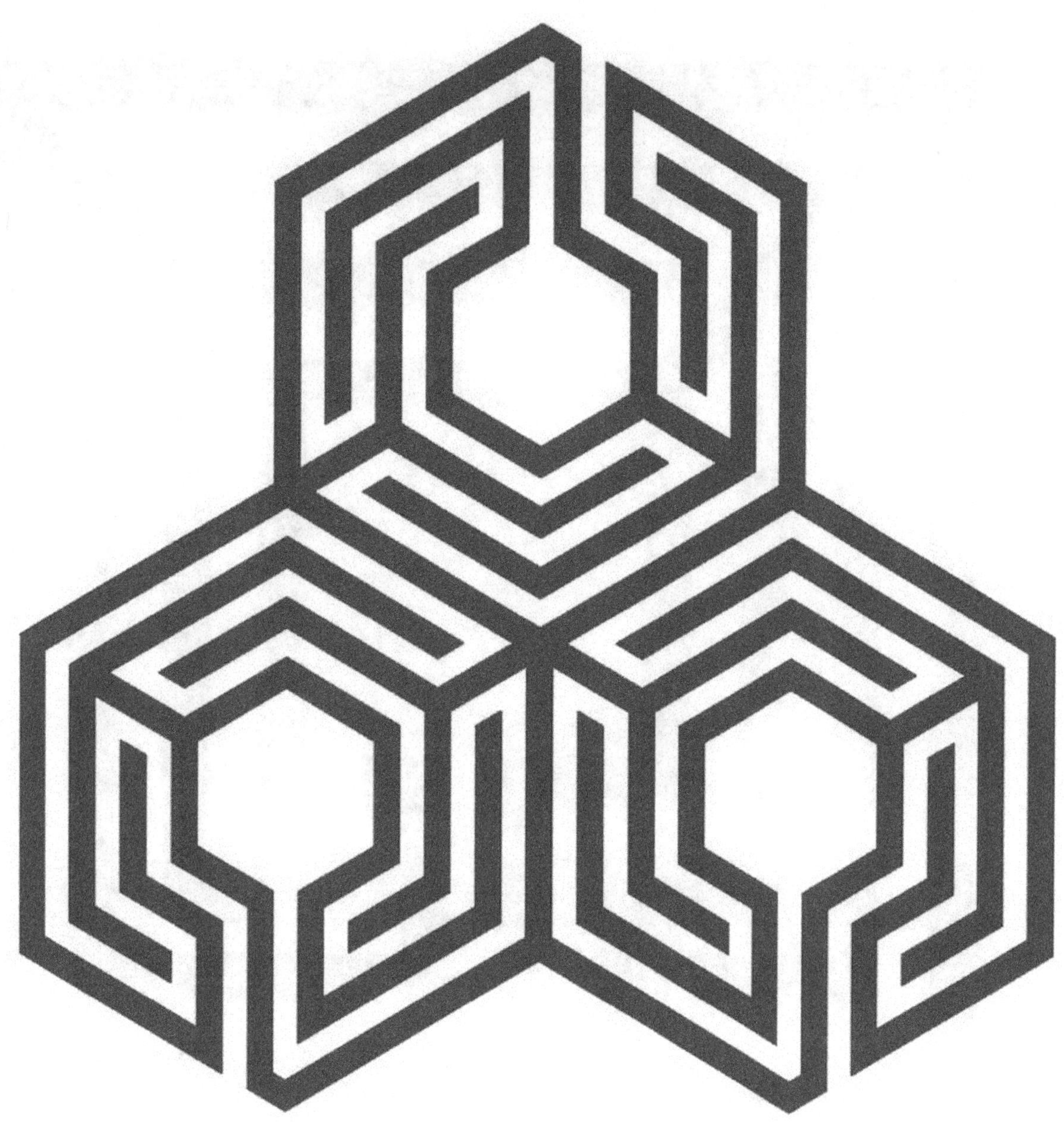

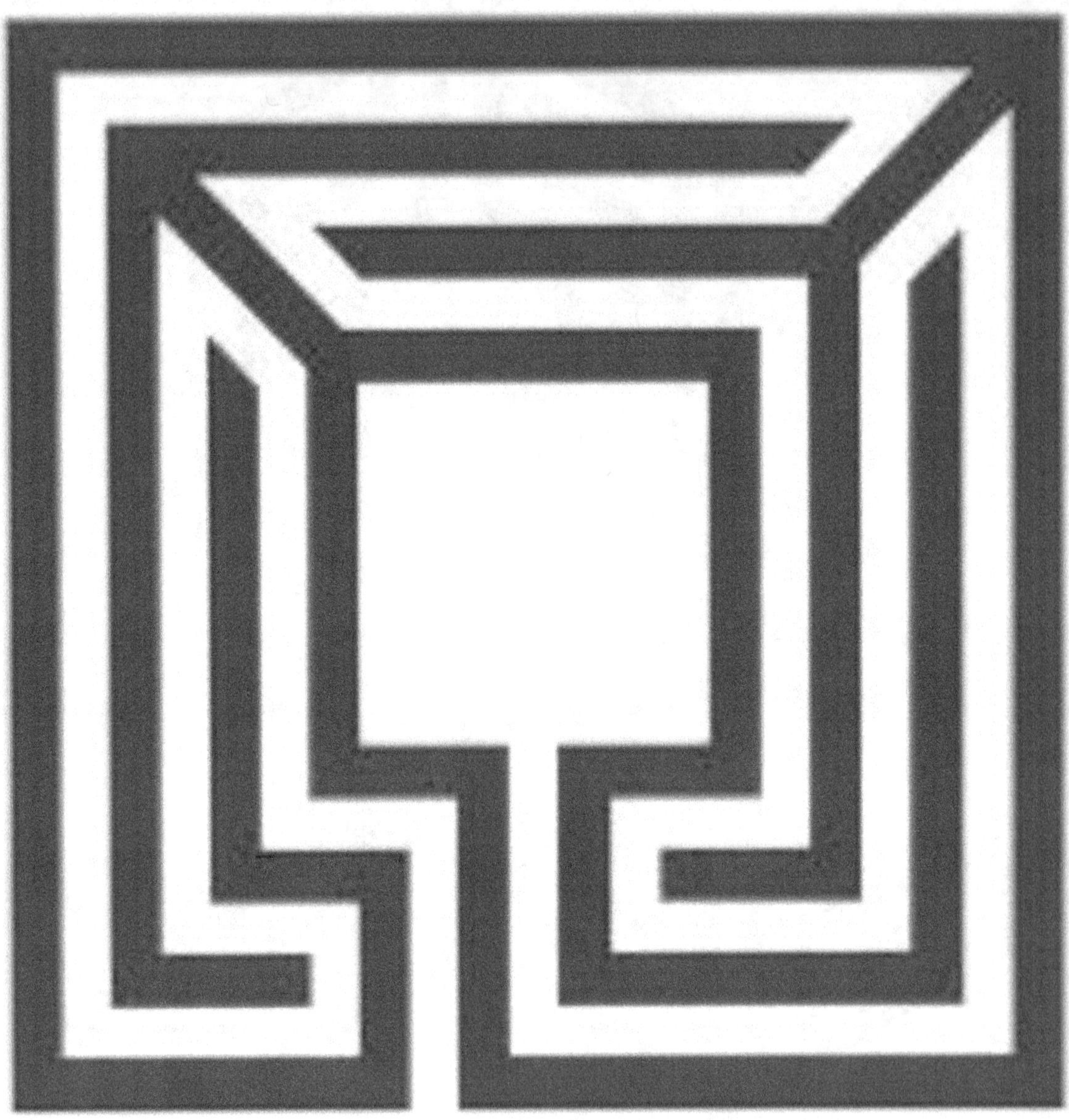

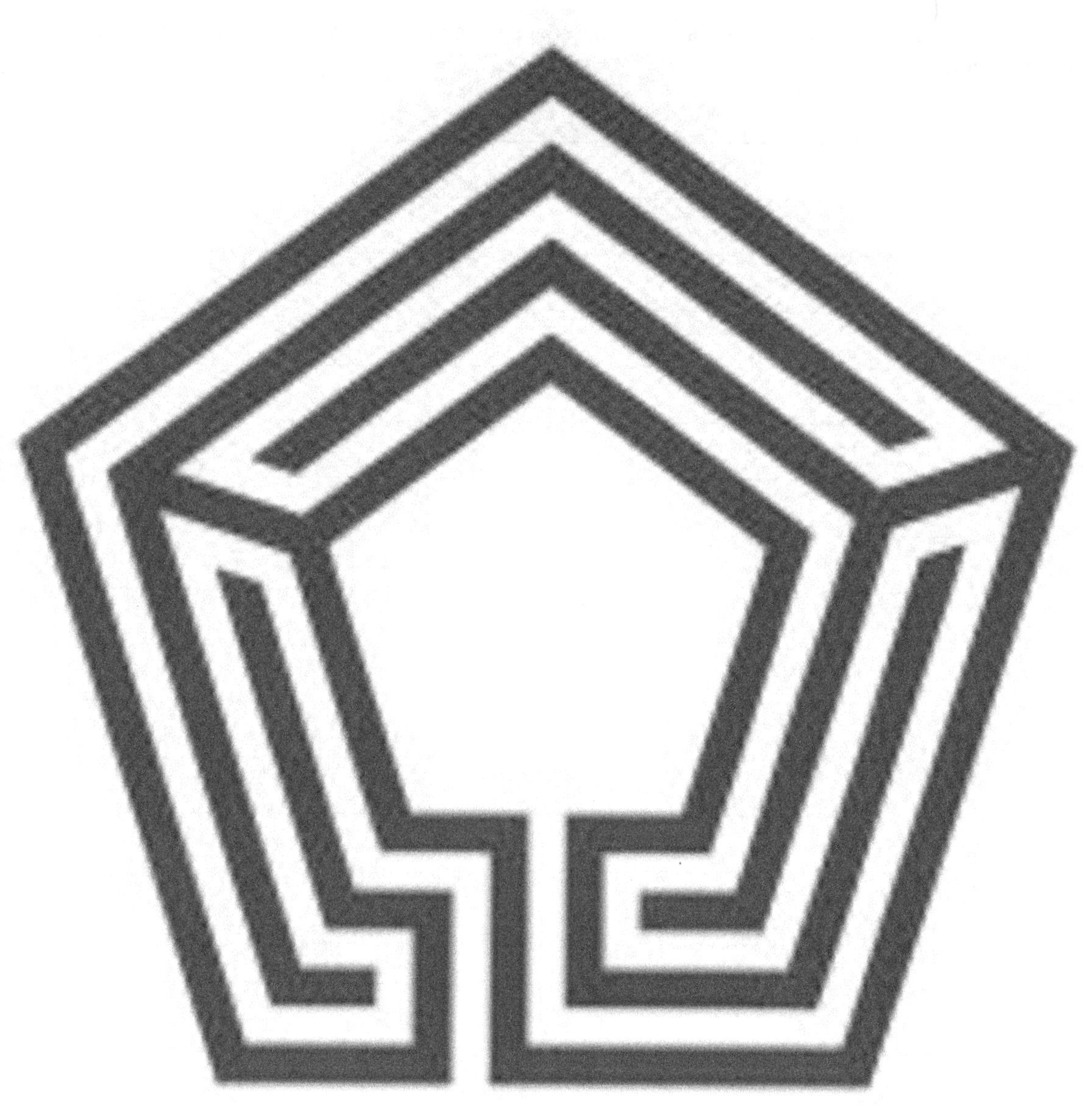

REFLECTIONS ON THIS BLOCK

Having walked the labyrinths in this block, what have you learned about your walk of faith? your relationship with God? ways in which you have difficulty being with the journey? parts of you that you hold back from fully engaging? lessons you are learning? Use this space to record your reflections on your journeys or arising from your journeys.

THIRD BLOCK

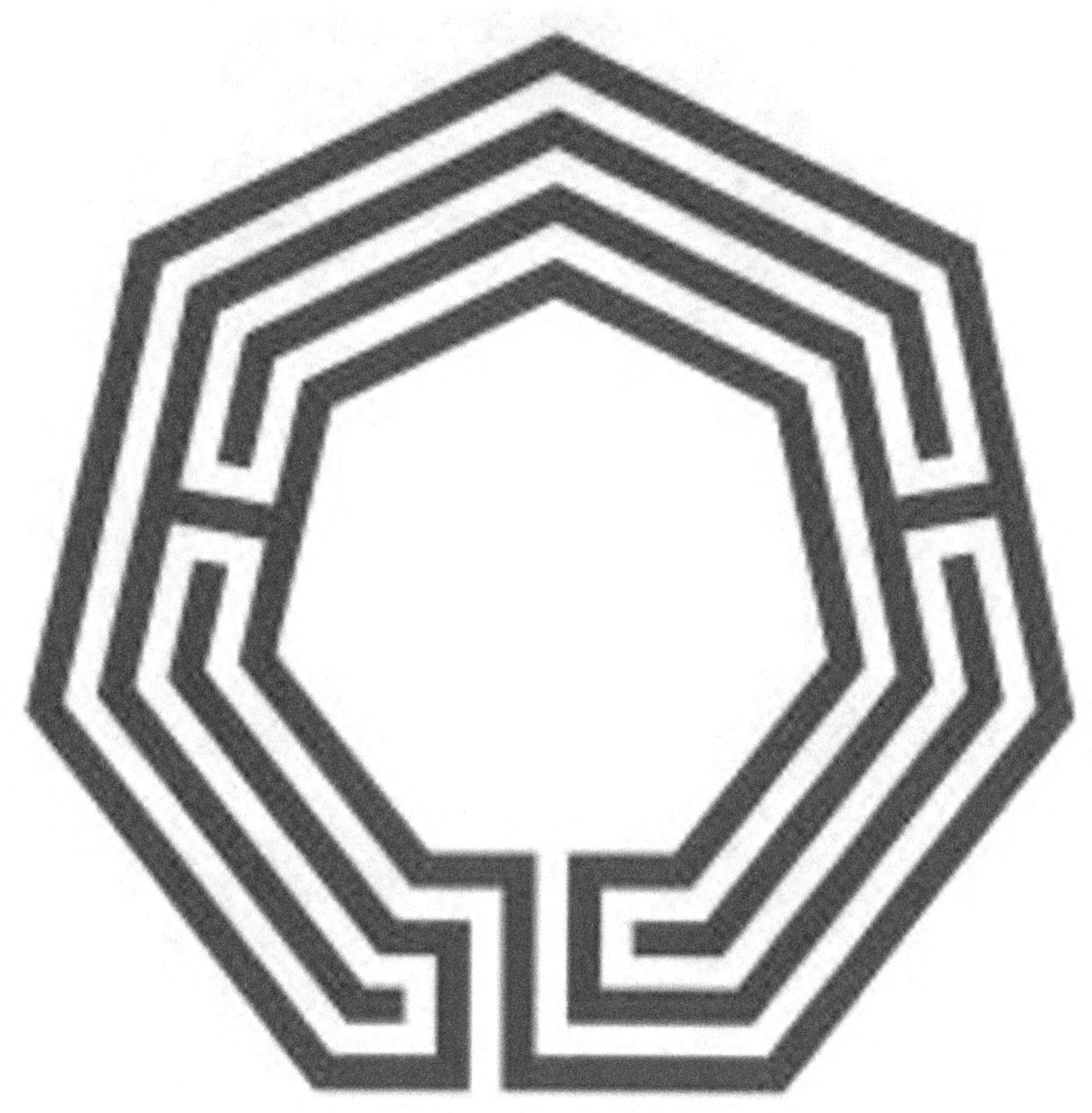

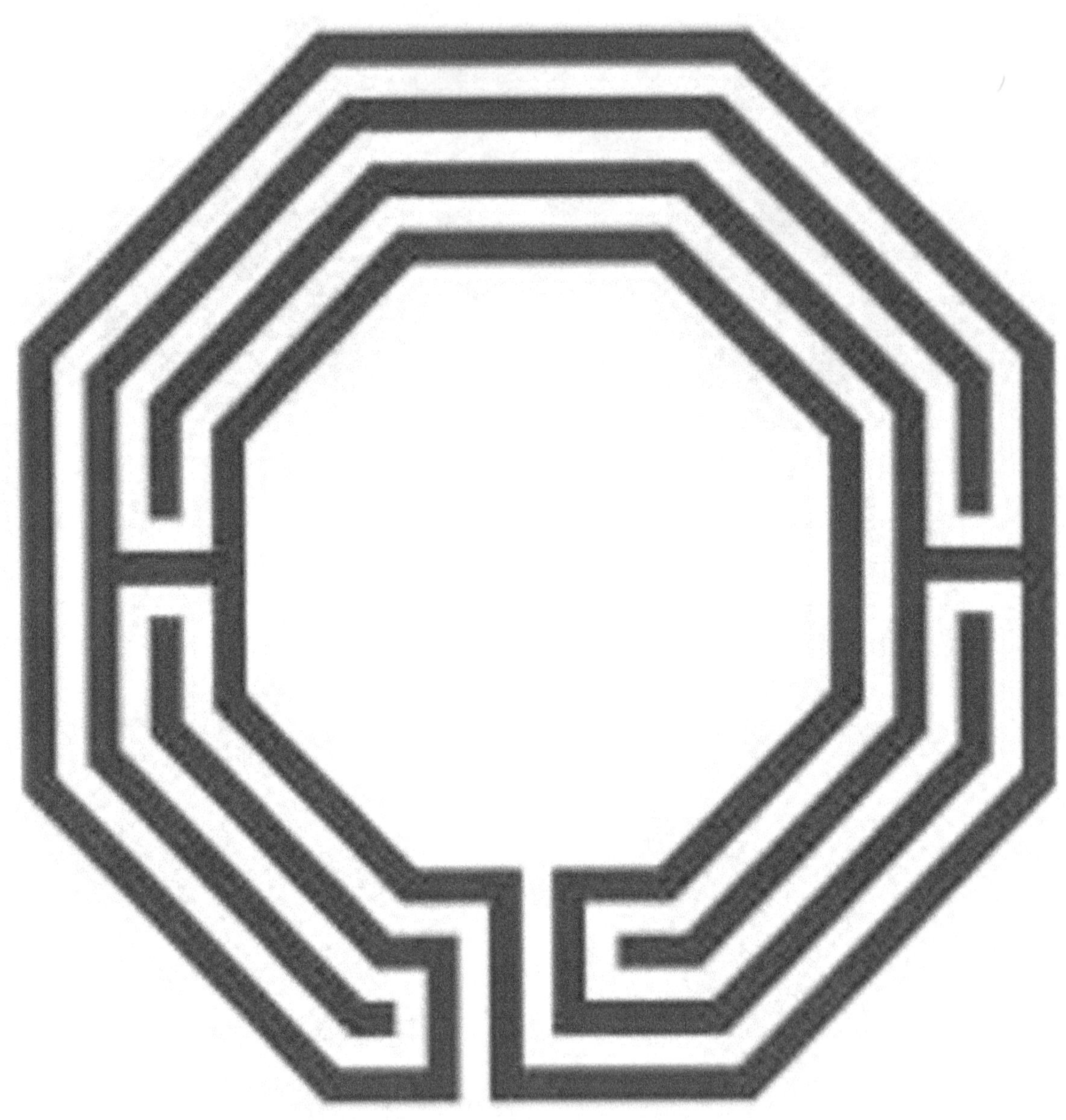

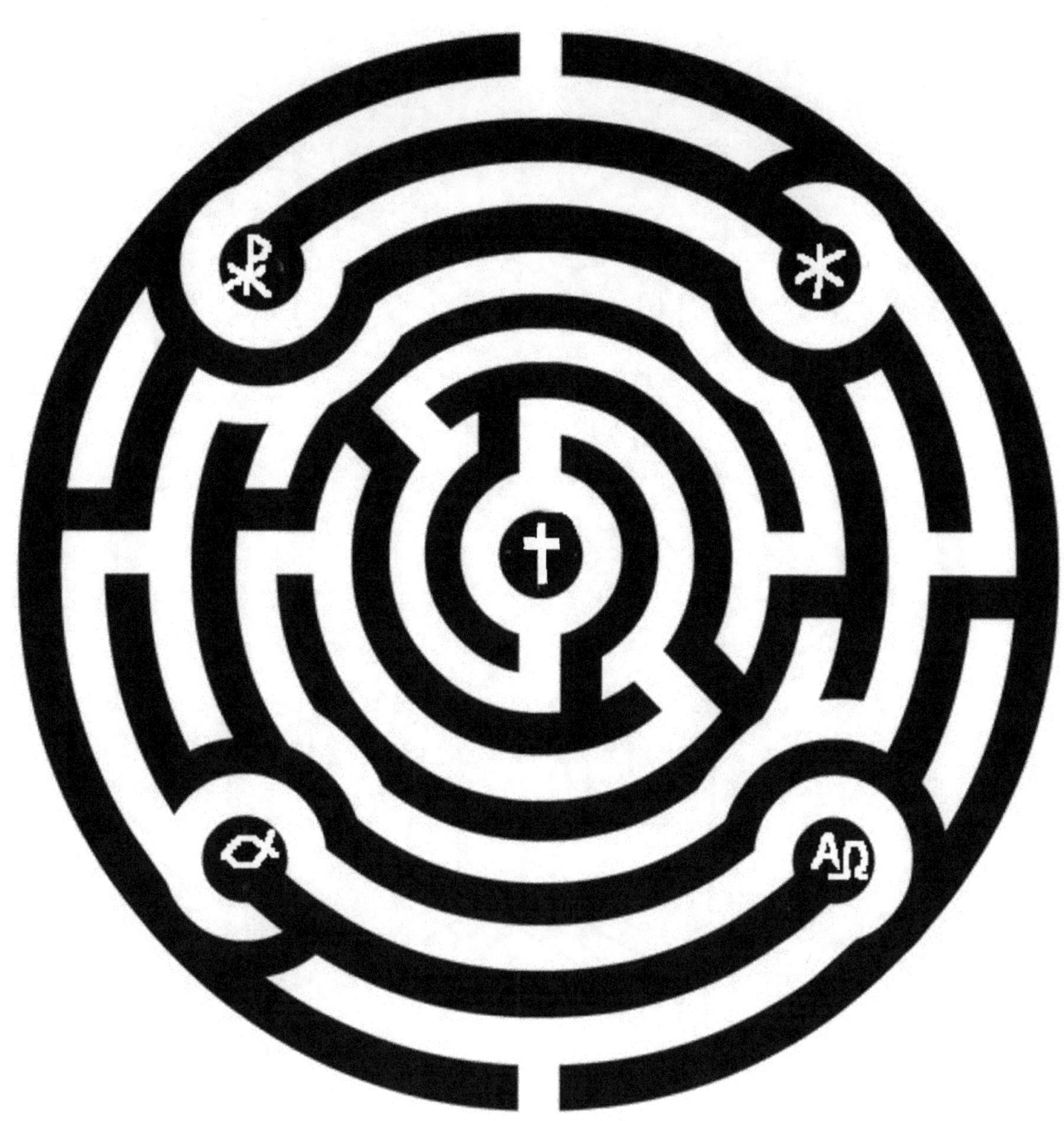
AΩ

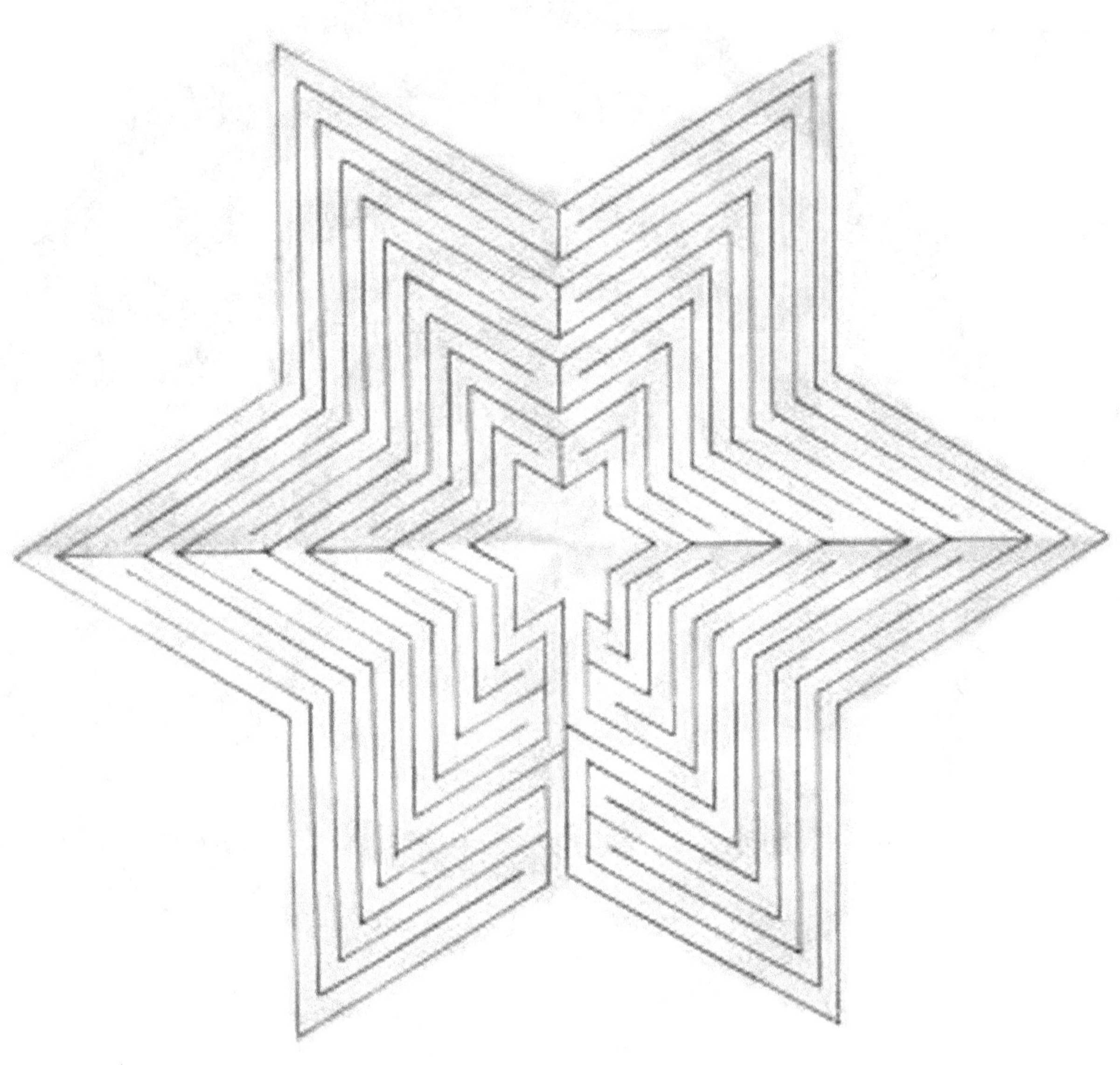

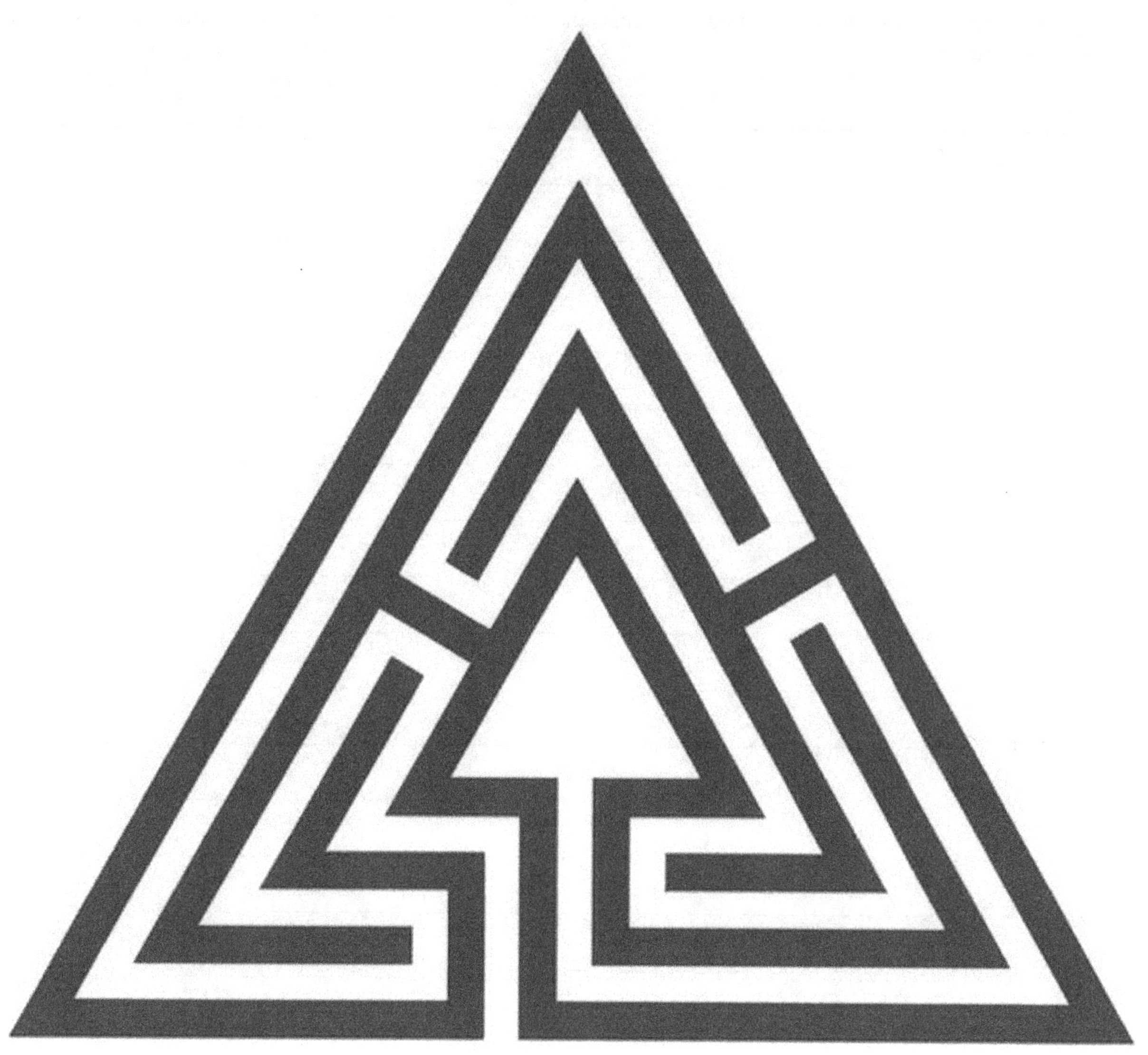

REFLECTIONS ON THIS BLOCK

Having walked the labyrinths in this block, what have you learned about your walk of faith? your relationship with God? ways in which you have difficulty being with the journey? parts of you that you hold back from fully engaging? lessons you are learning? Use this space to record your reflections on your journeys or arising from your journeys.

FOURTH BLOCK

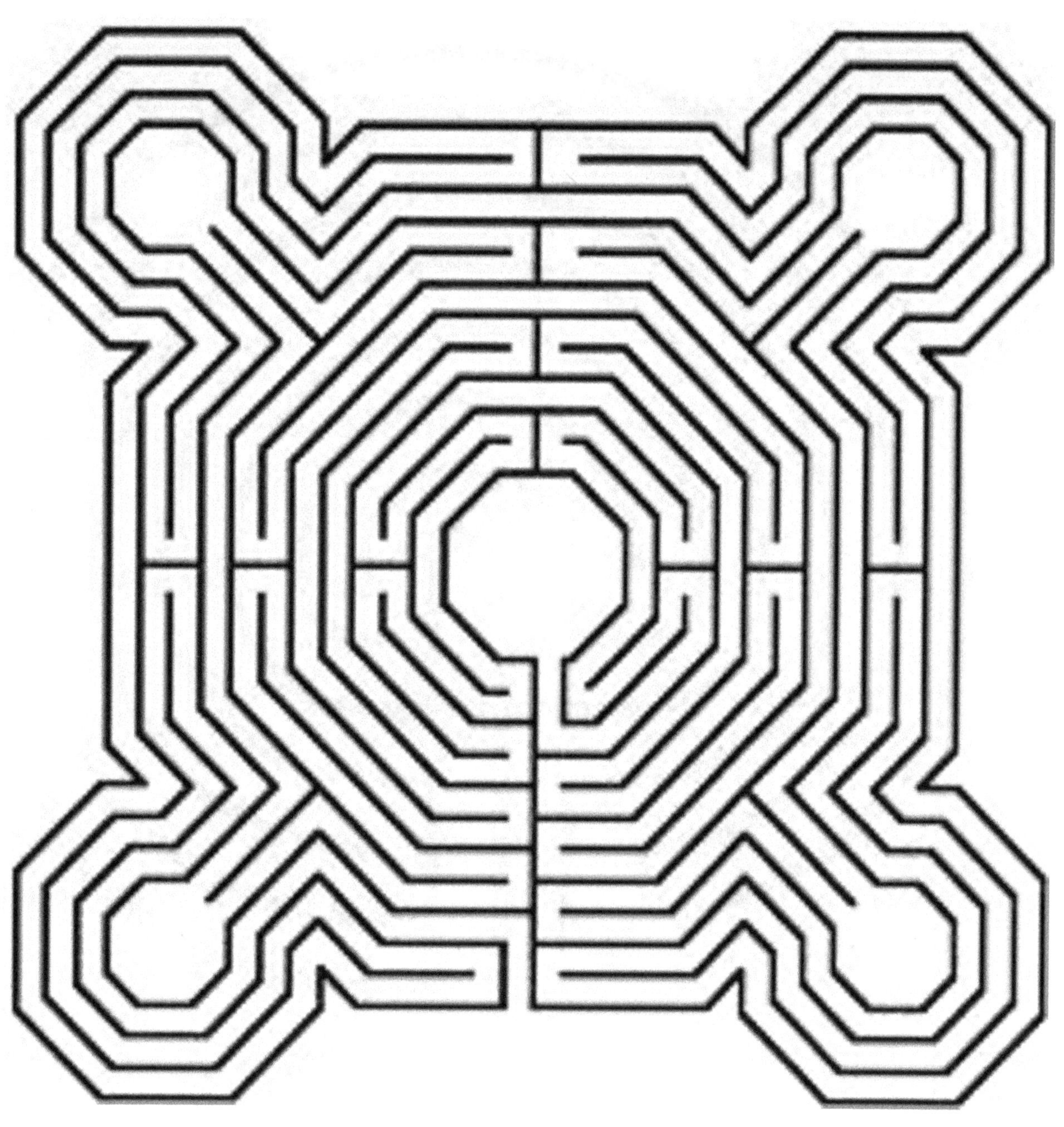

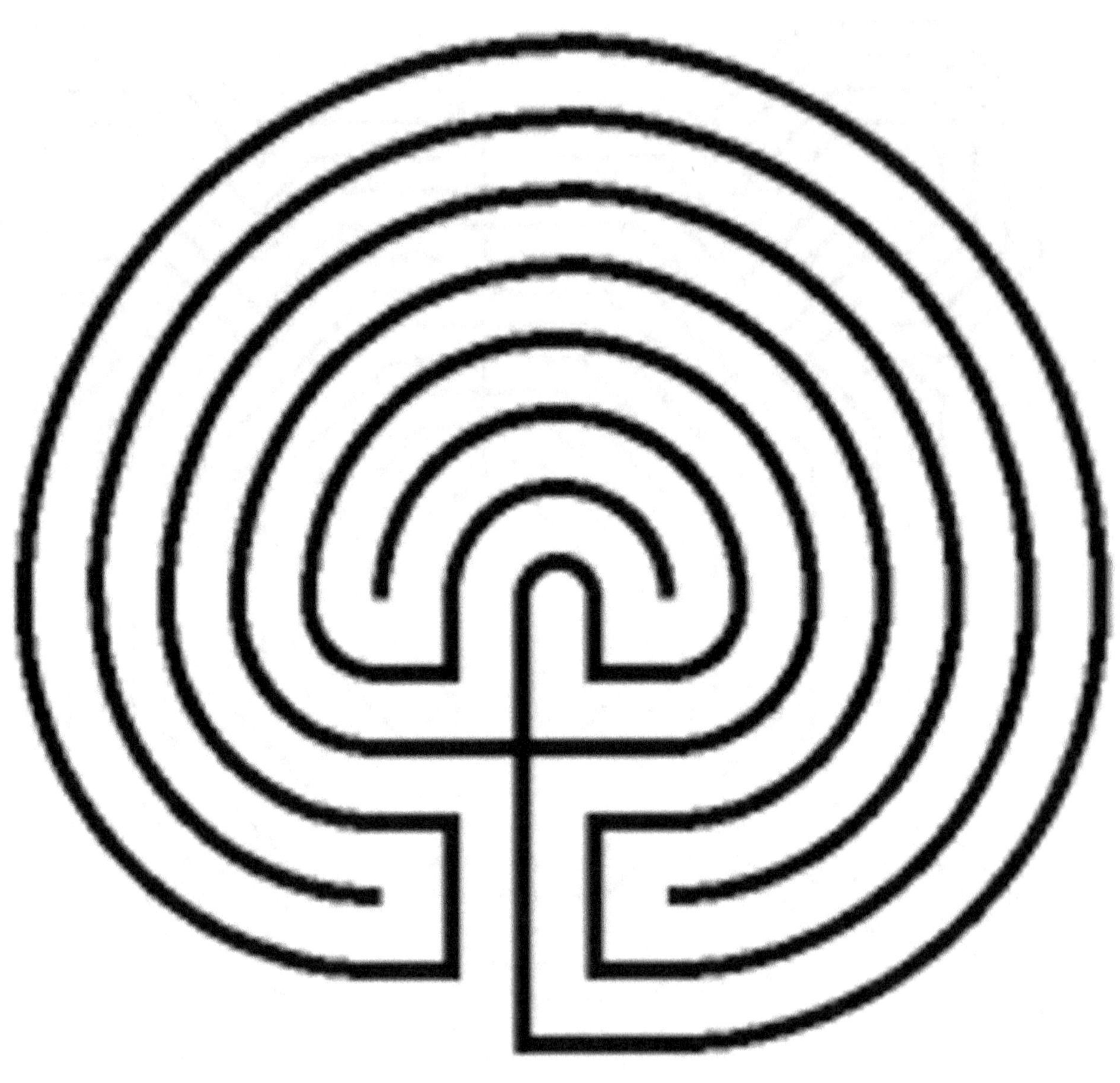

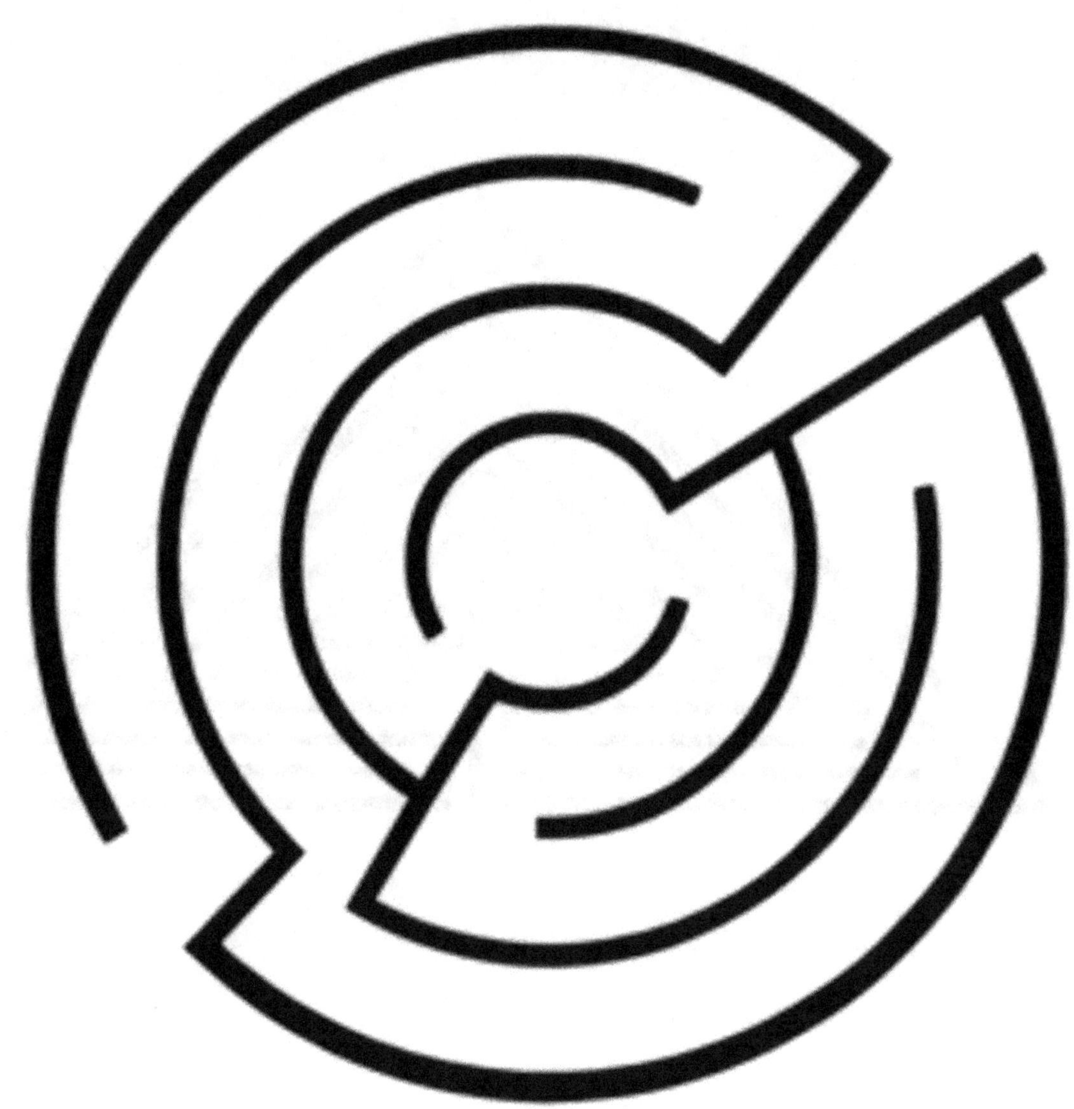

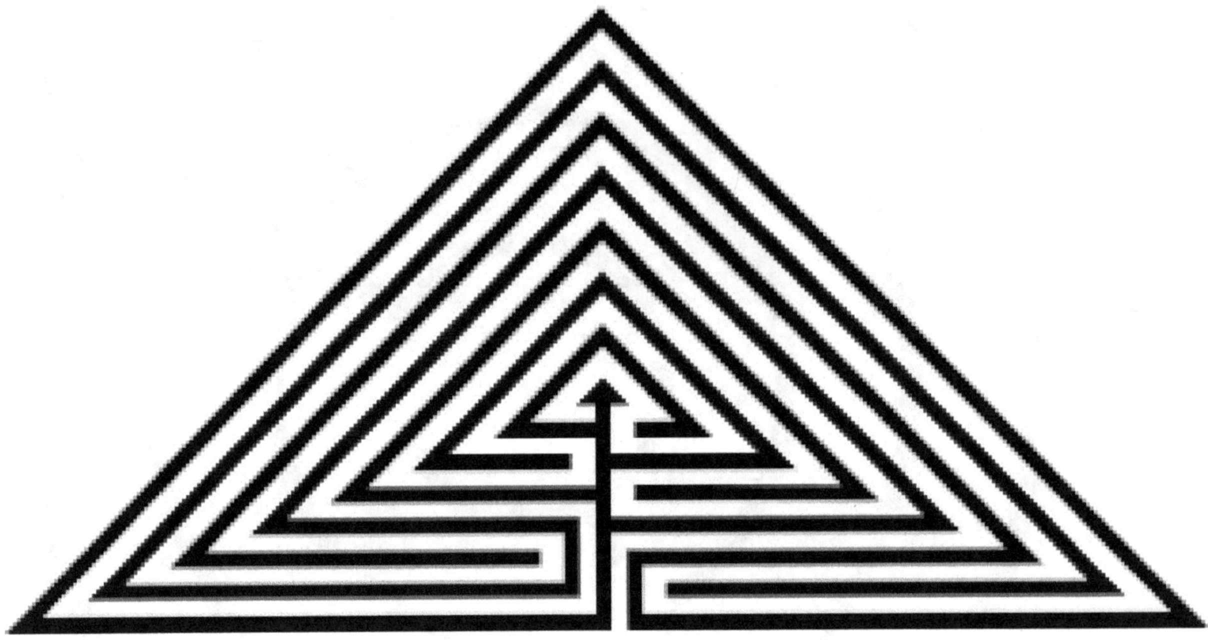

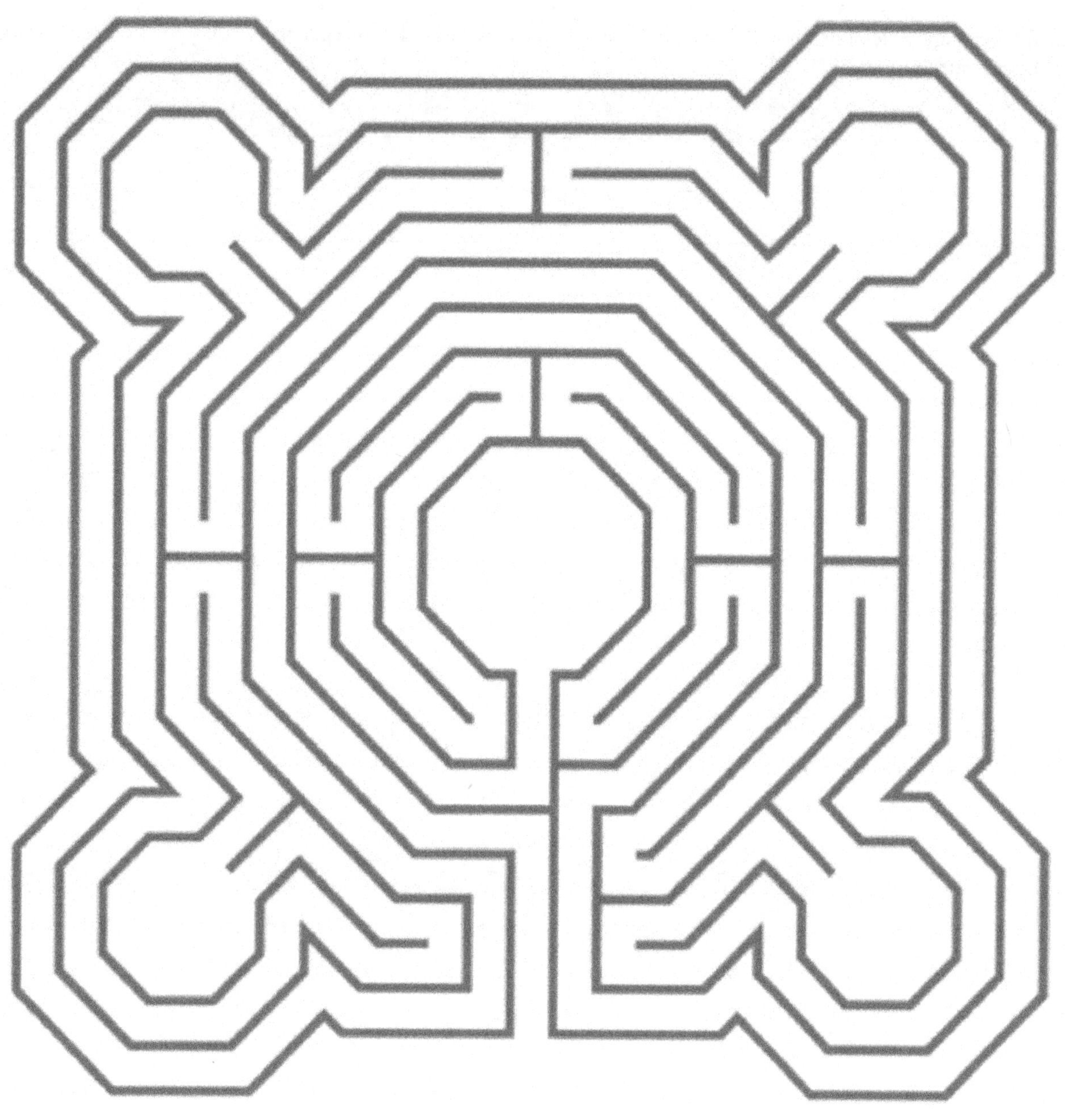

REFLECTIONS ON THIS BLOCK

Having walked the labyrinths in this block, what have you learned about your walk of faith? your relationship with God? ways in which you have difficulty being with the journey? parts of you that you hold back from fully engaging? lessons you are learning? Use this space to record your reflections on your journeys or arising from your journeys.

FIFTH BLOCK

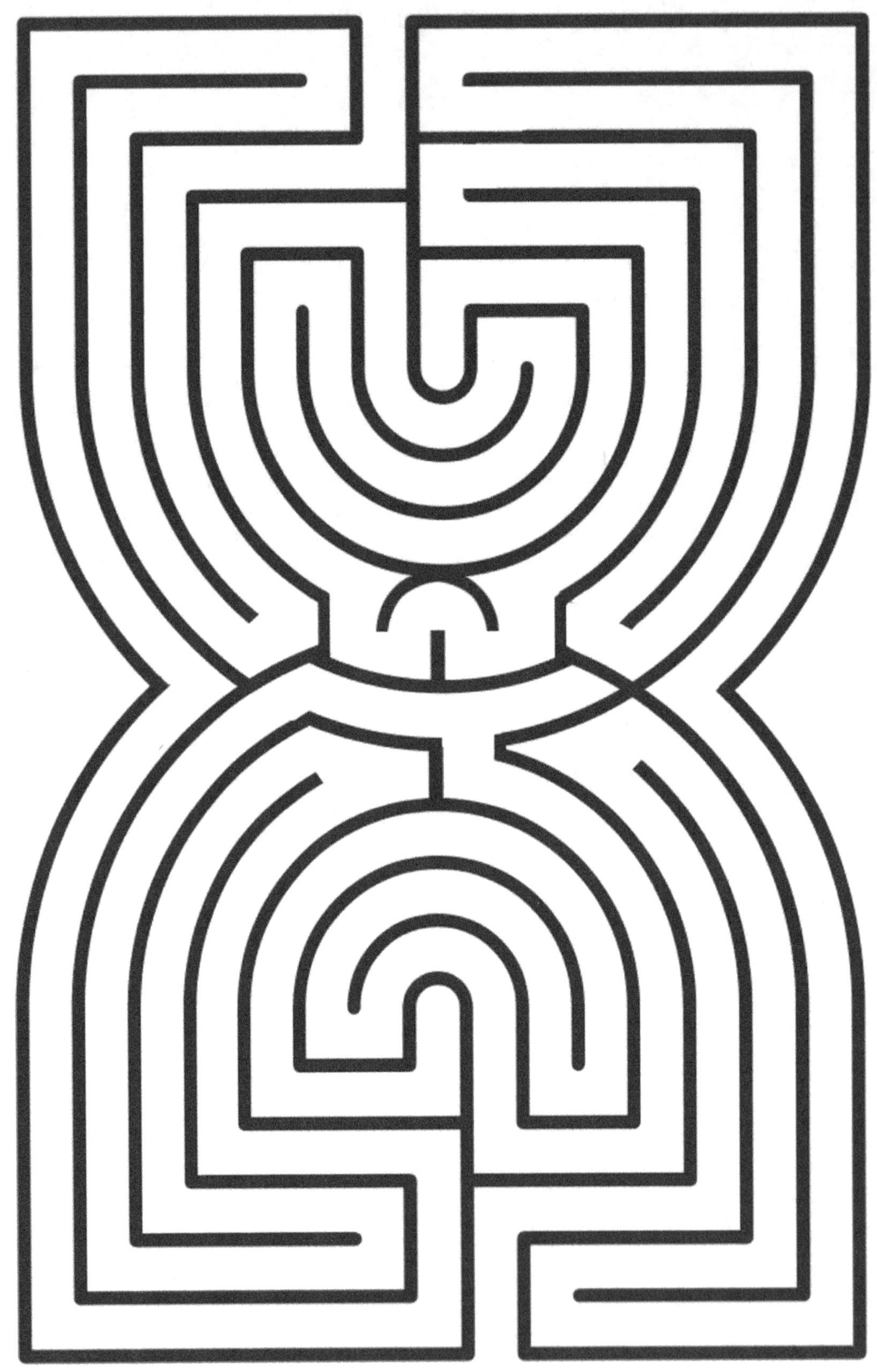

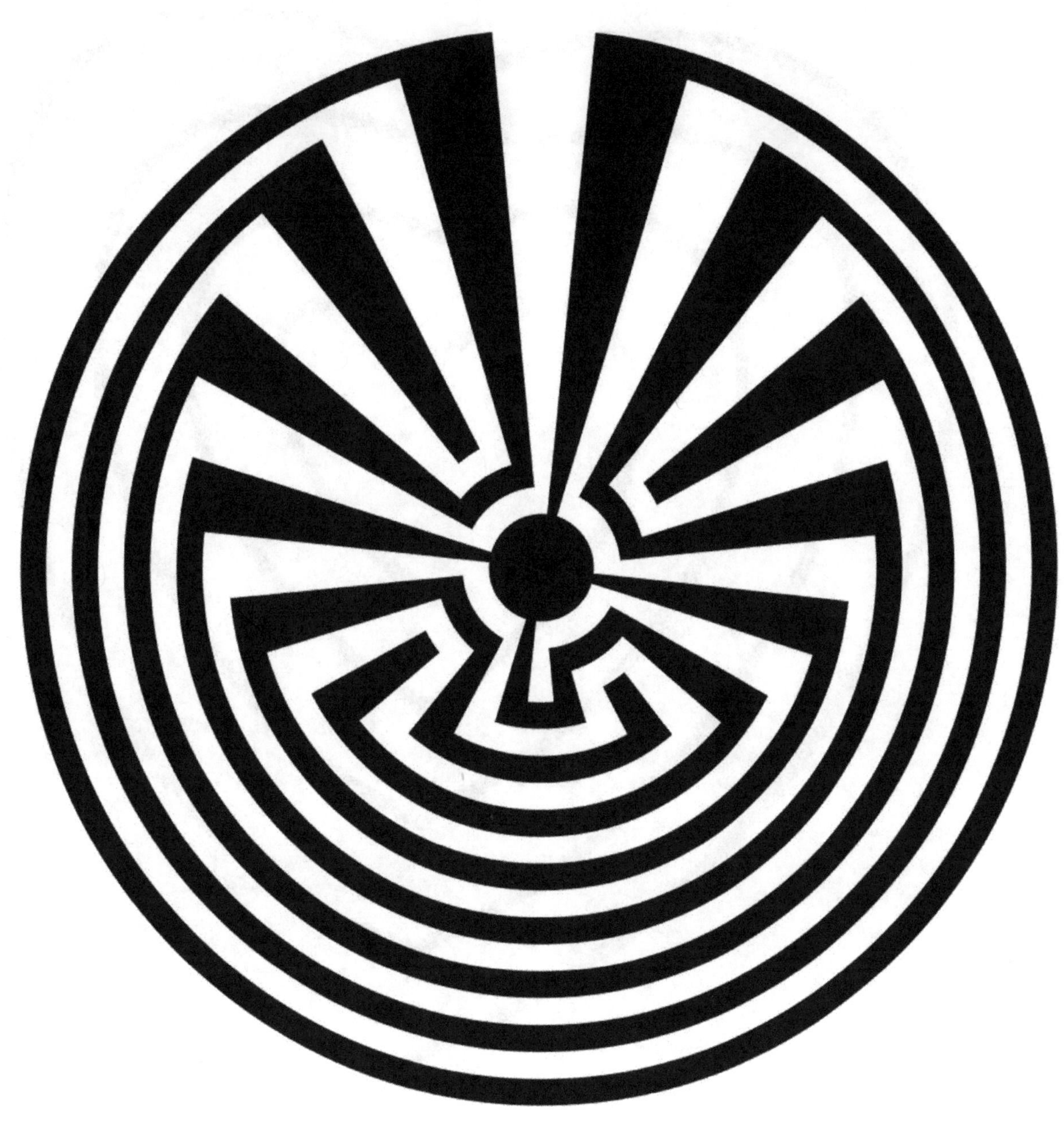

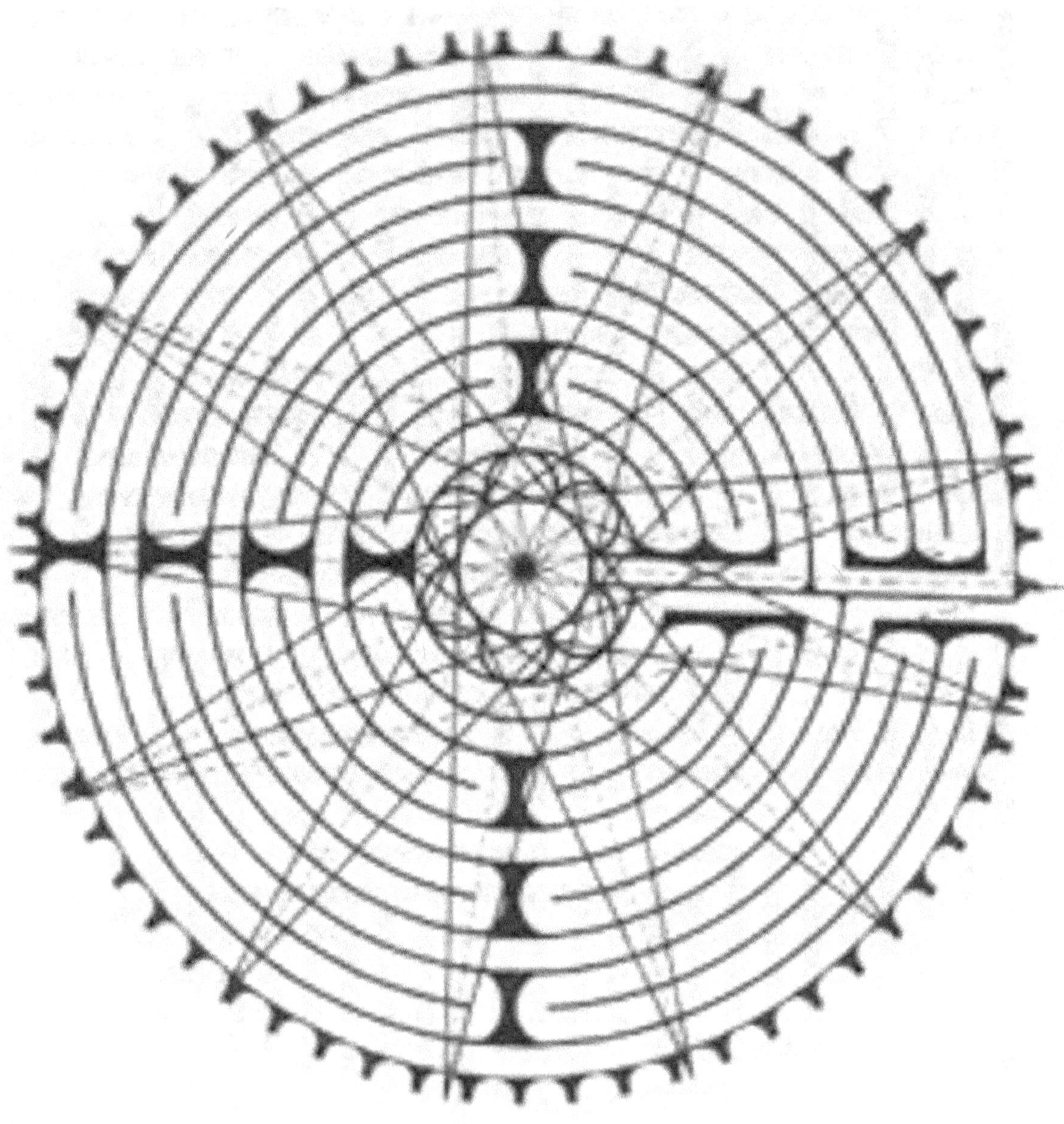

REFLECTIONS ON THIS BLOCK

Having walked the labyrinths in this block, what have you learned about your walk of faith? your relationship with God? ways in which you have difficulty being with the journey? parts of you that you hold back from fully engaging? lessons you are learning? Use this space to record your reflections on your journeys or arising from your journeys.

SIXTH BLOCK

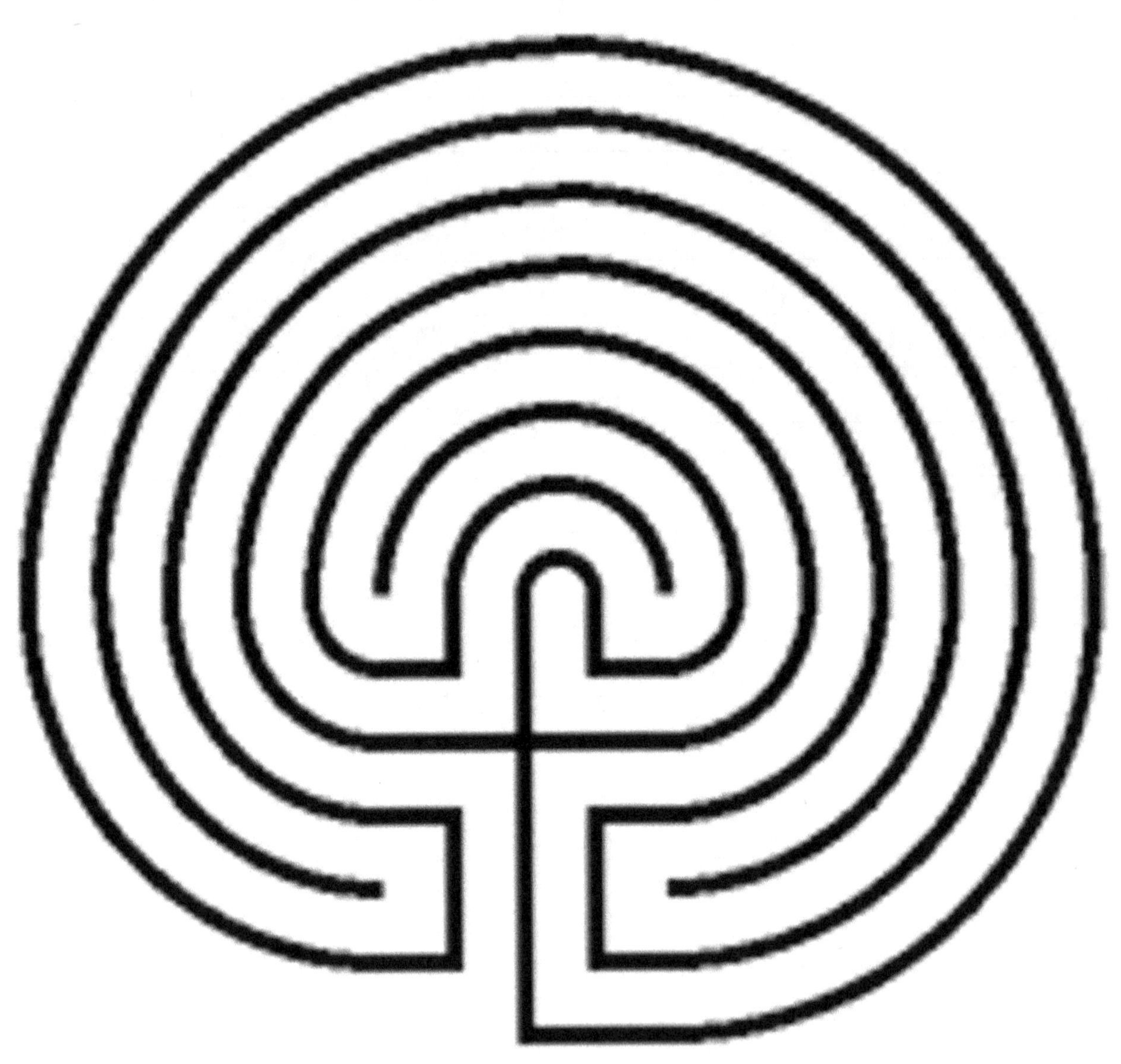

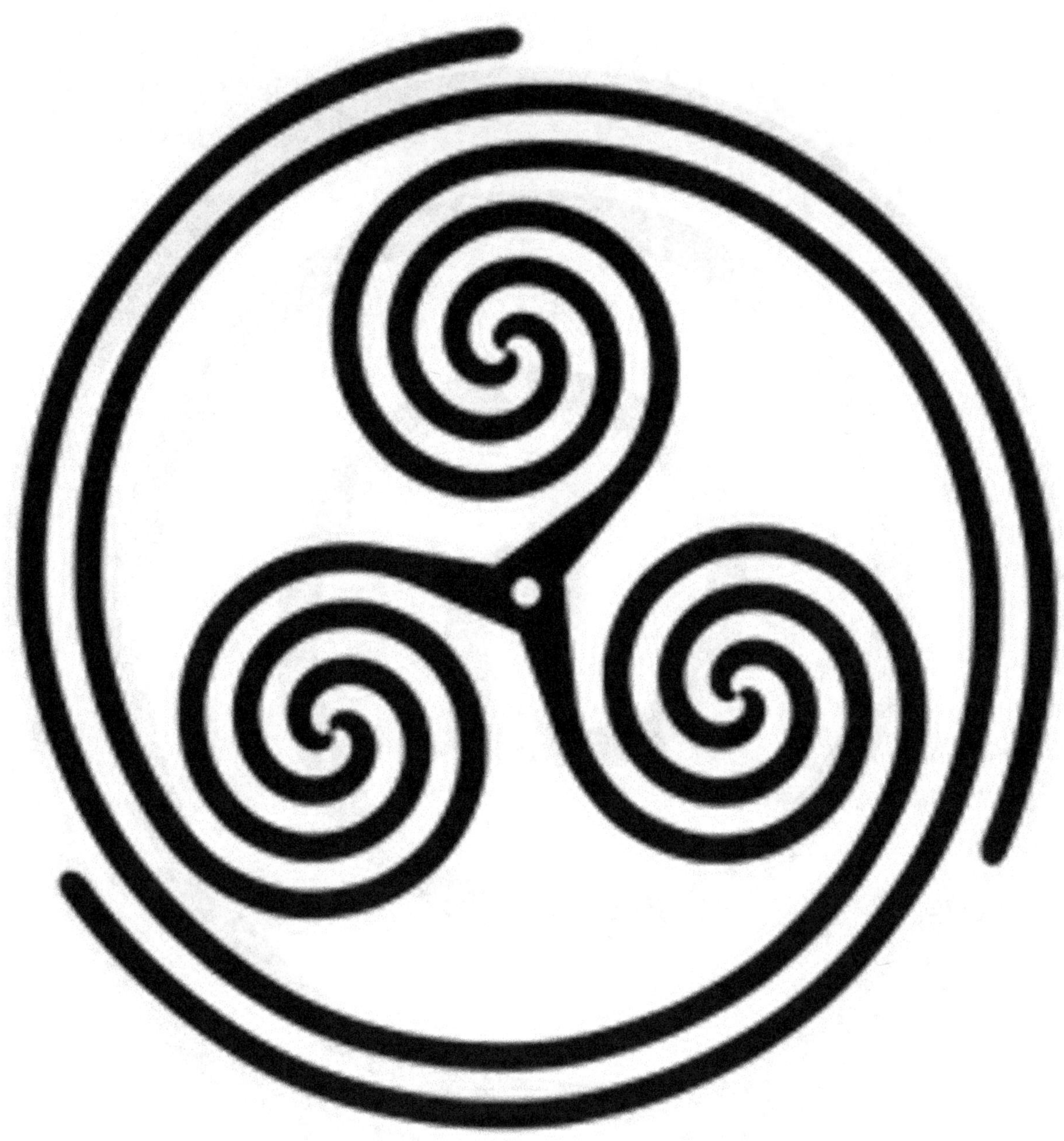

This one does not strictly have an entrance but you can see where to start.

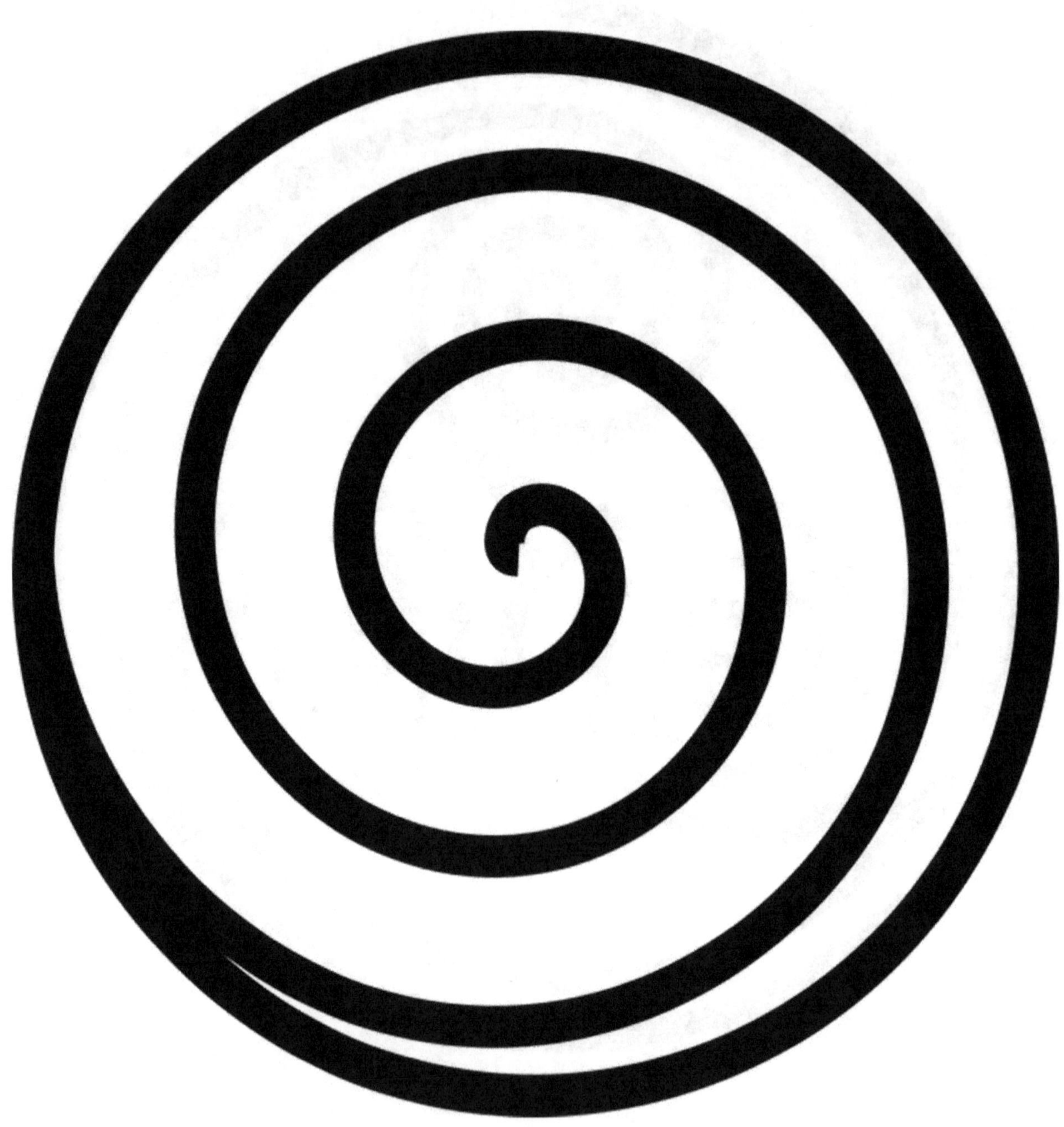

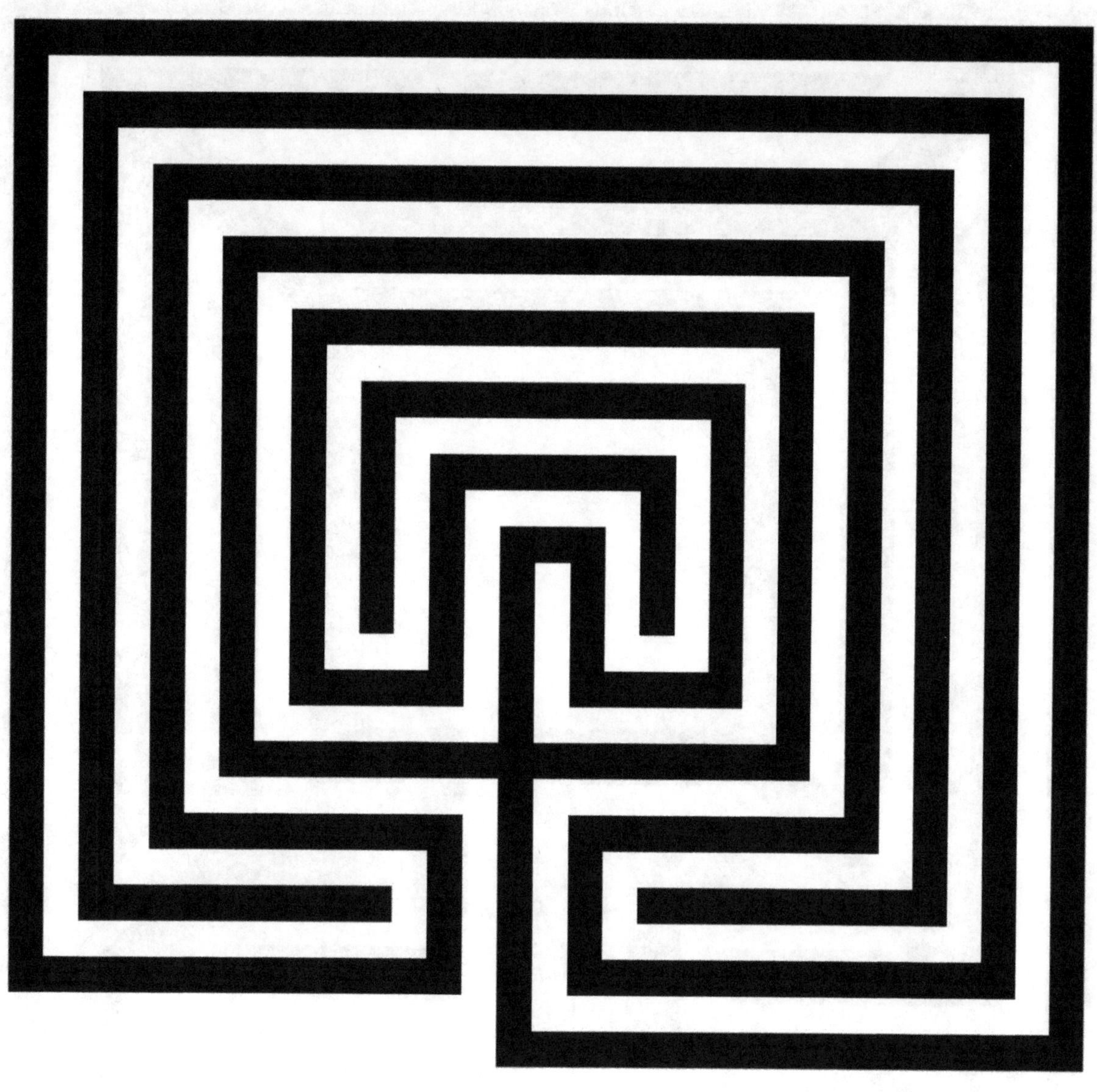

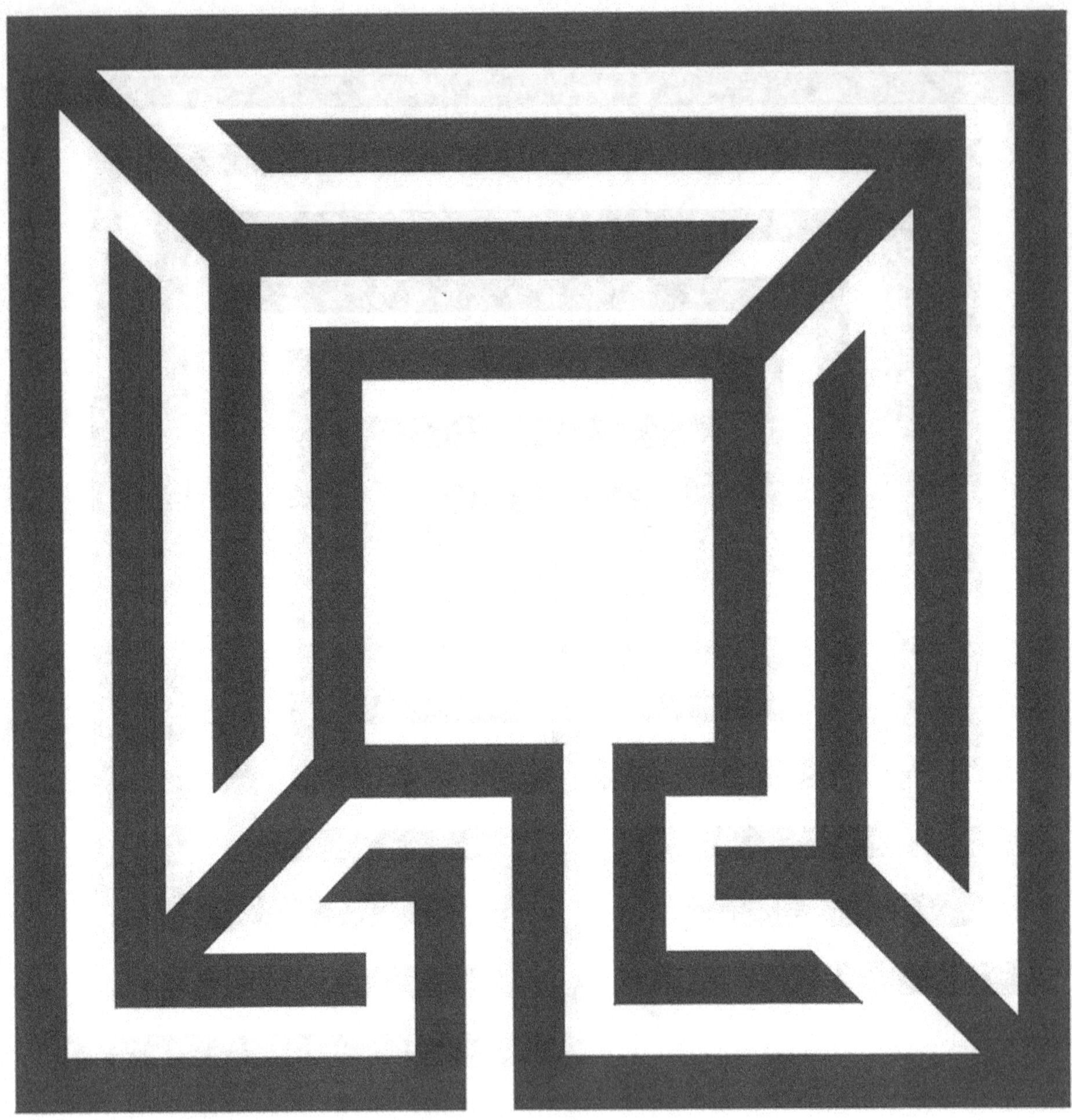

REFLECTIONS ON THIS BLOCK

Having walked the labyrinths in this block, what have you learned about your walk of faith? your relationship with God? ways in which you have difficulty being with the journey? parts of you that you hold back from fully engaging? lessons you are learning? Use this space to record your reflections on your journeys or arising from your journeys.

SEVENTH BLOCK

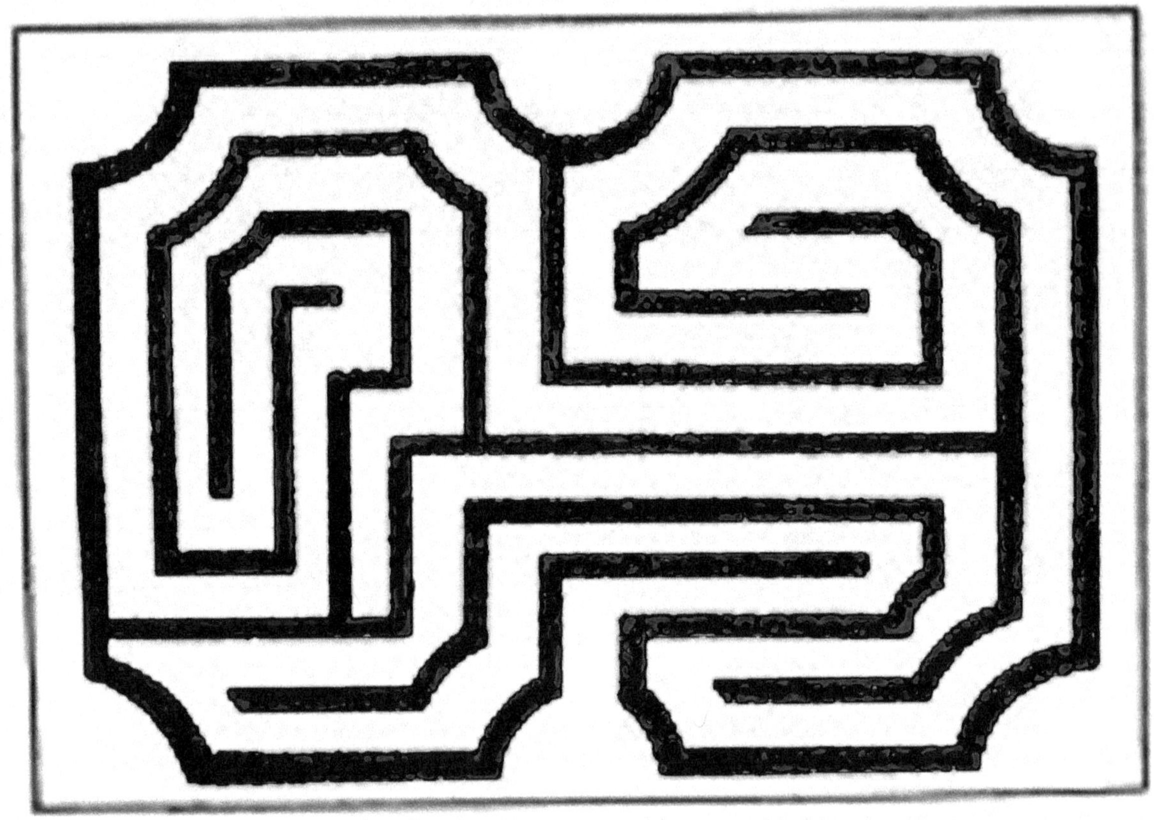

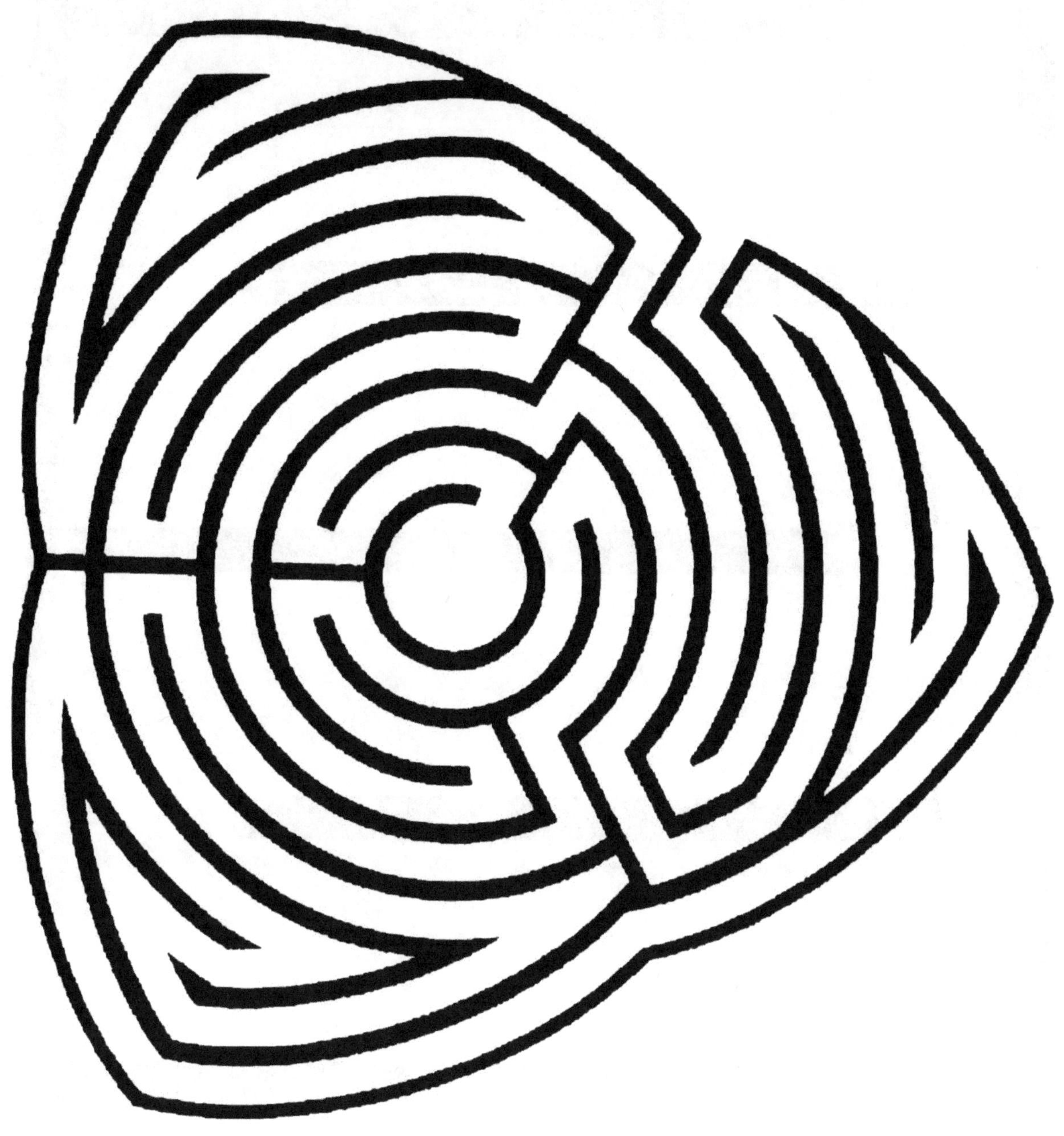

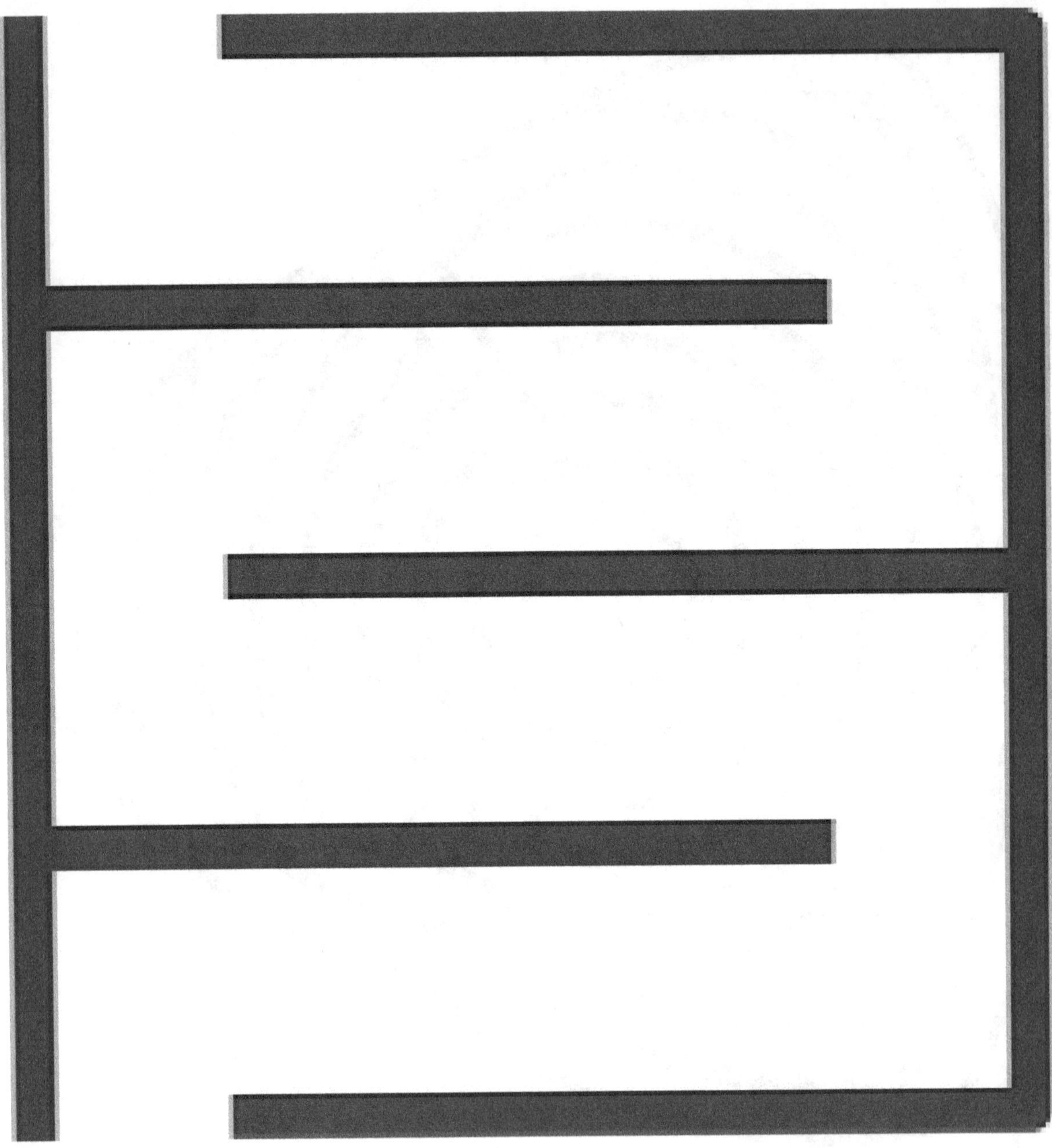

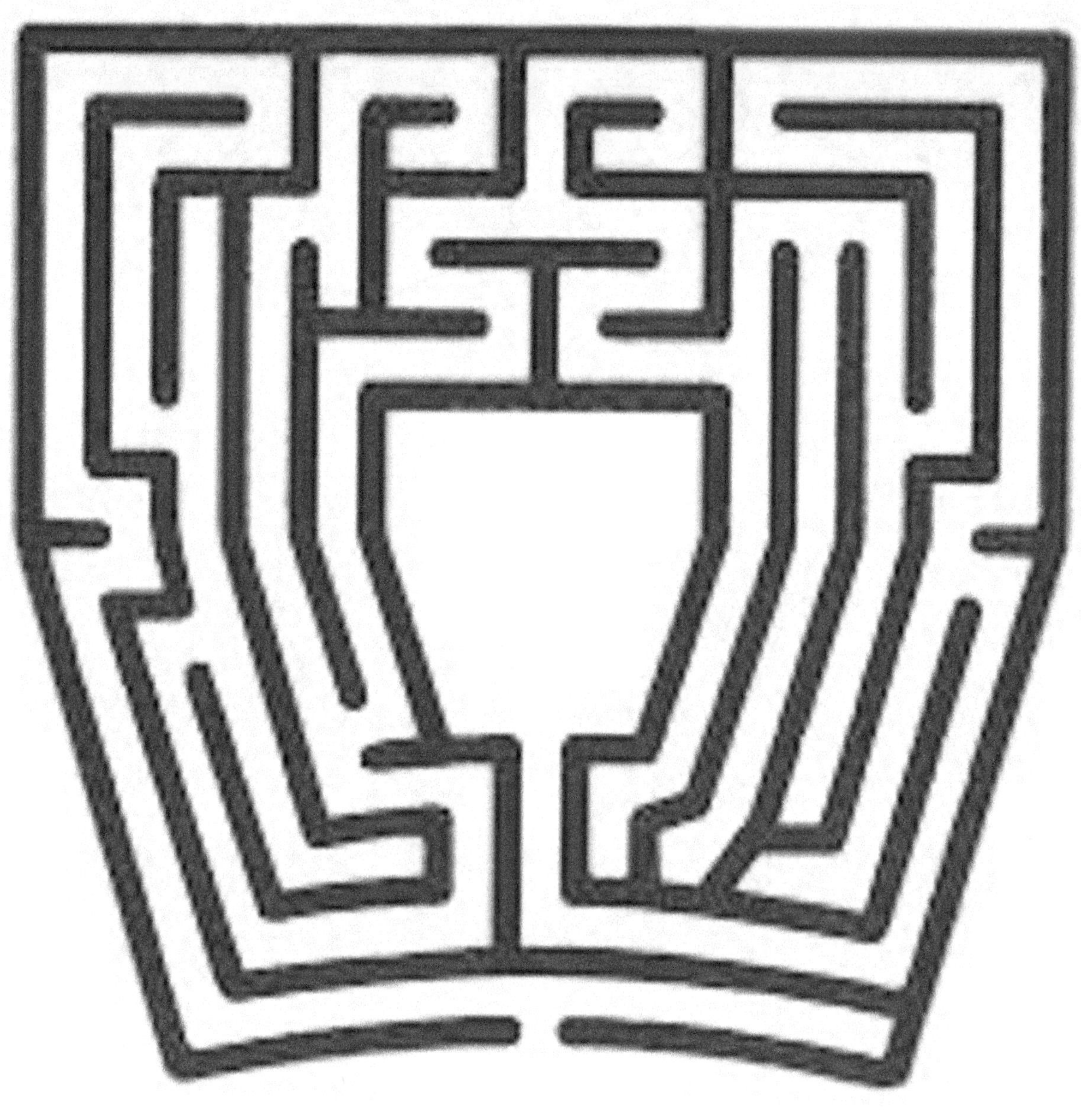

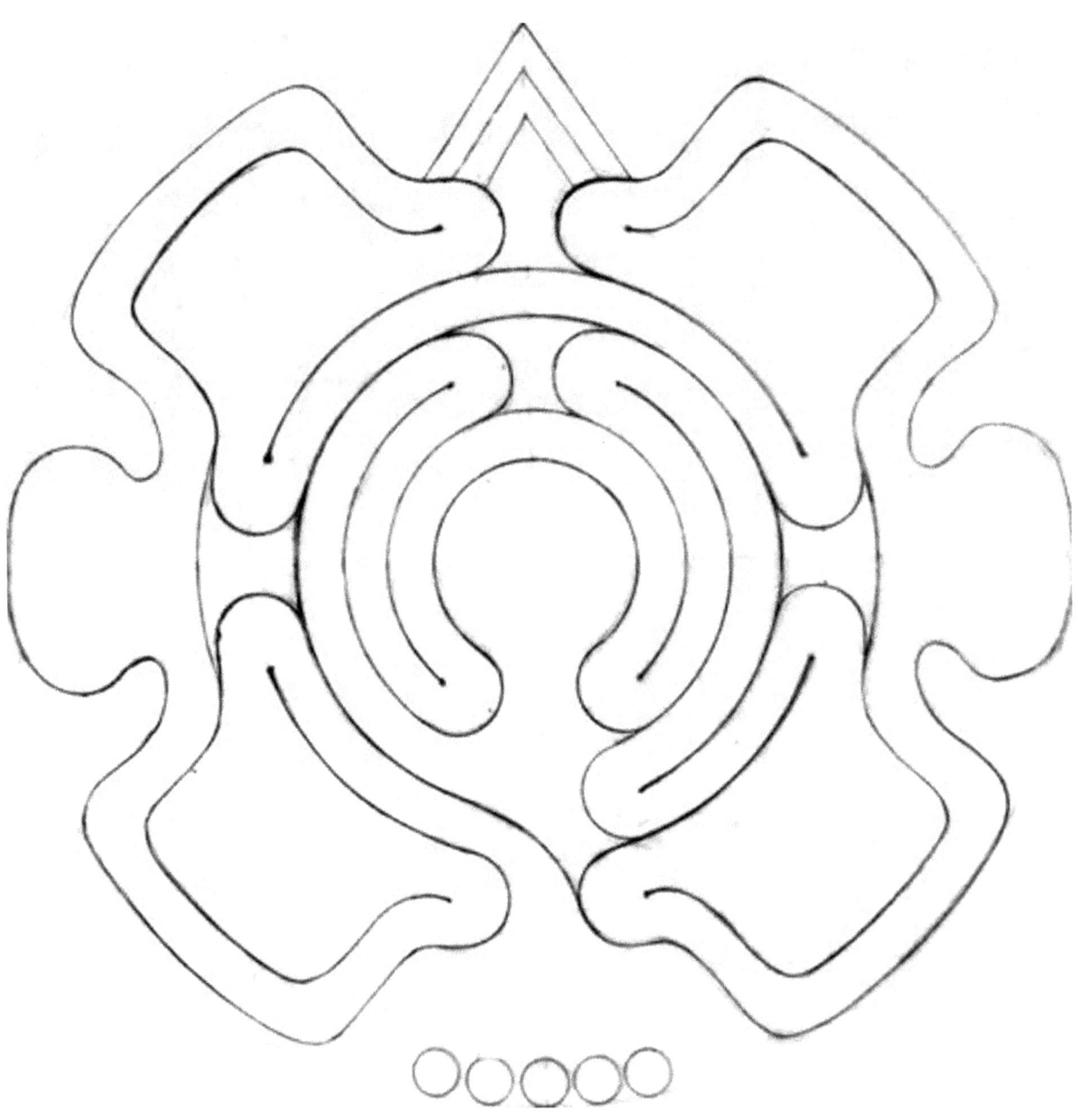

REFLECTIONS ON THIS BLOCK

Having walked the labyrinths in this block, what have you learned about your walk of faith? your relationship with God? ways in which you have difficulty being with the journey? parts of you that you hold back from fully engaging? lessons you are learning? Use this space to record your reflections on your journeys or arising from your journeys.

EIGHTH BLOCK

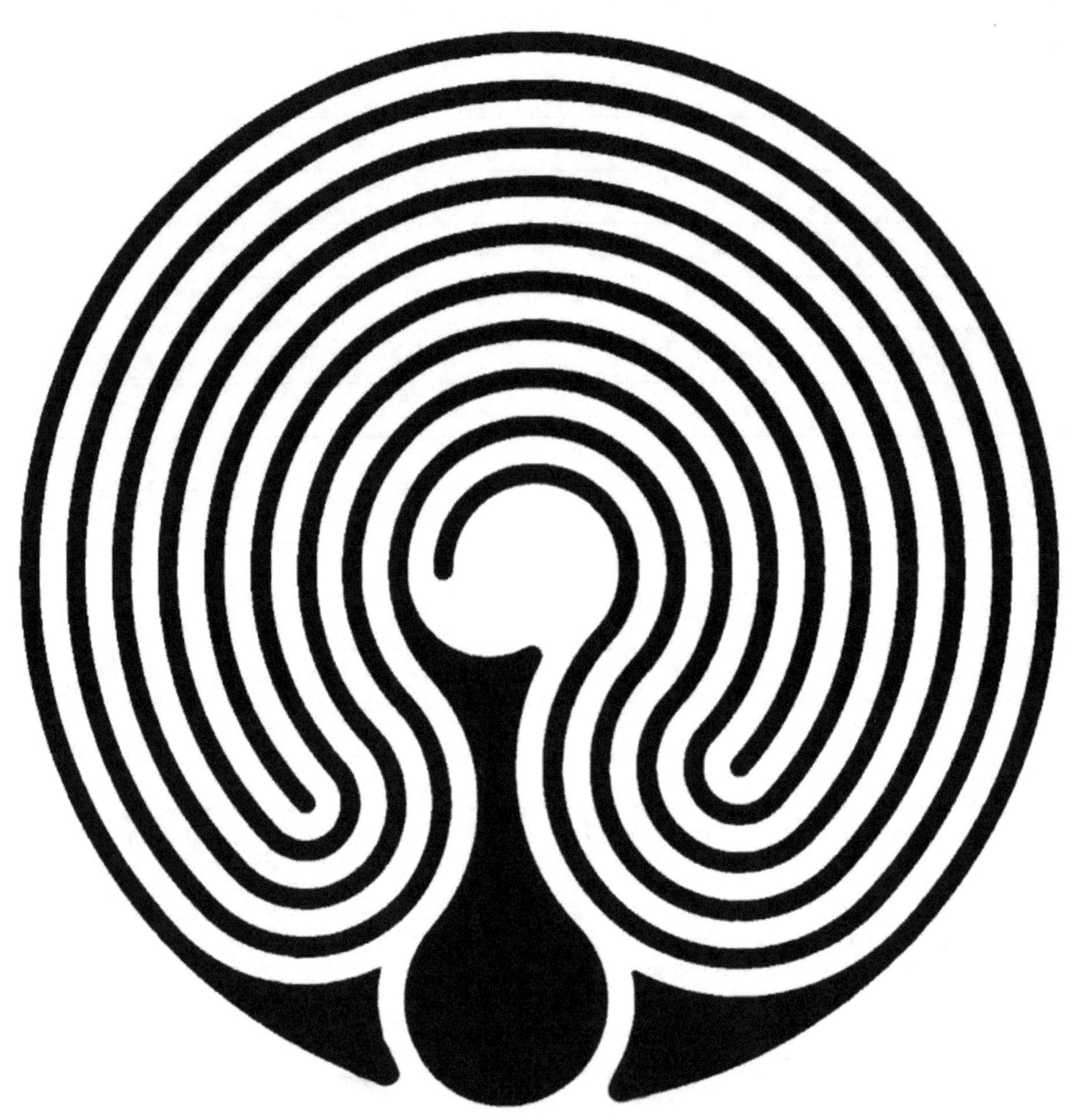

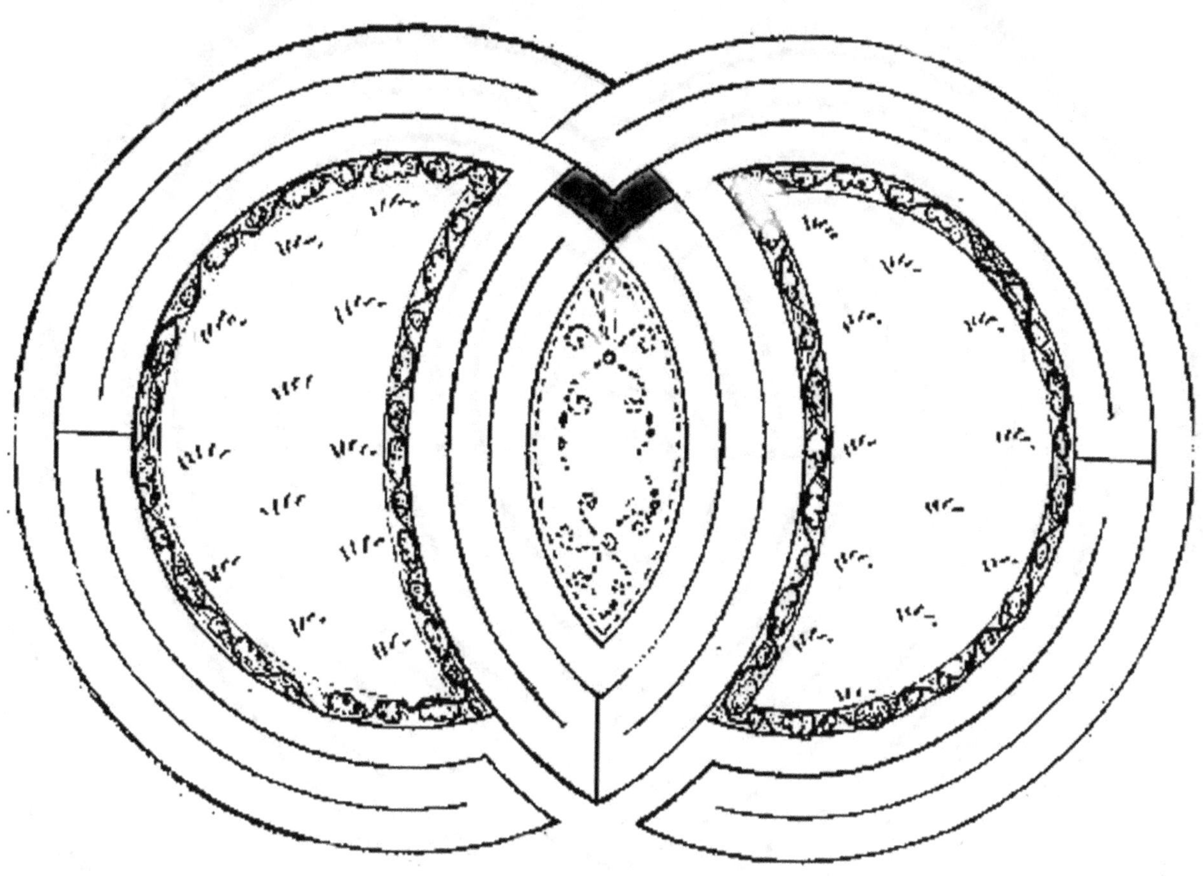

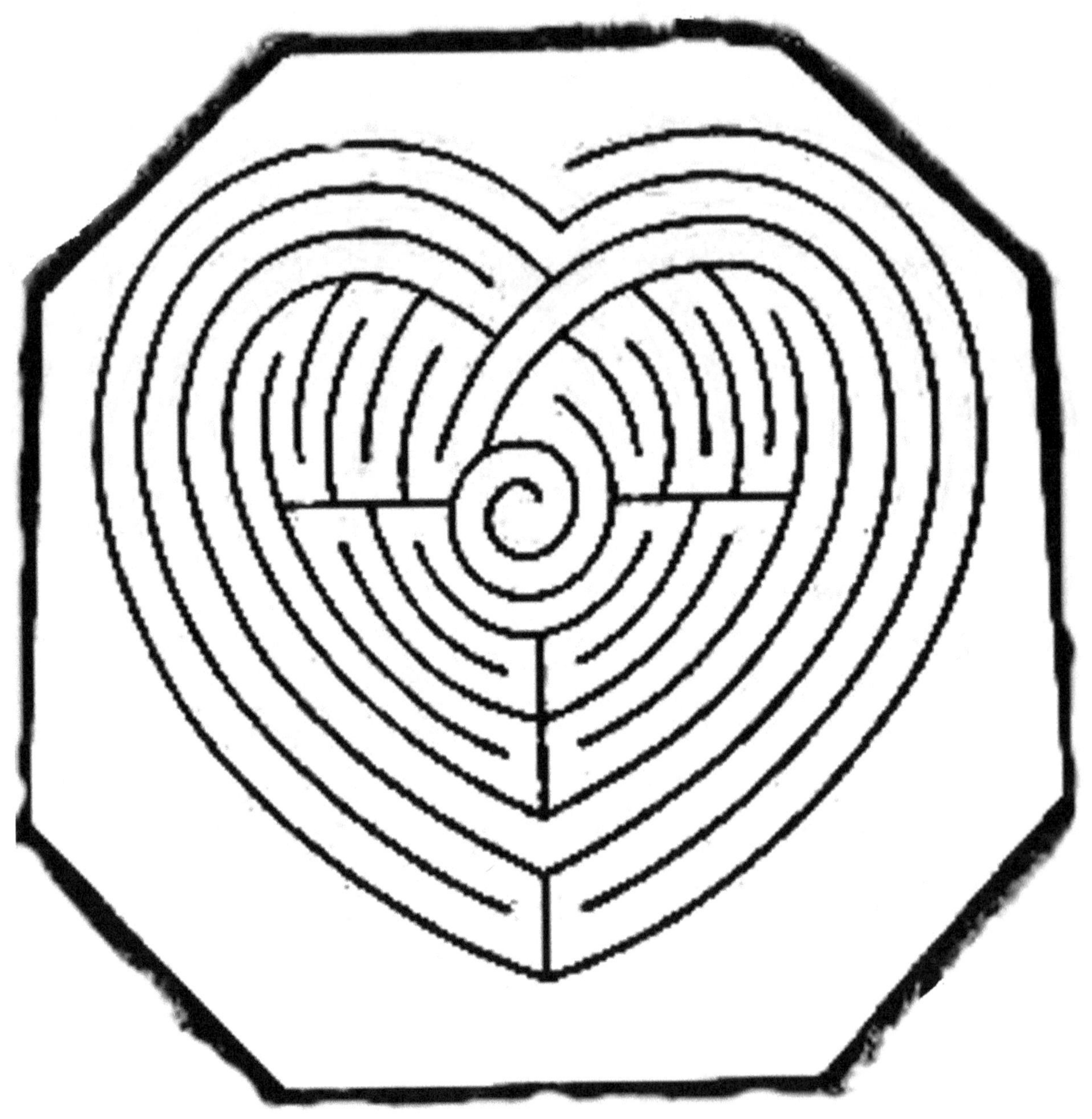

If you are up to the challenge, now that you have done many labyrinths and have just one more to go, if you want, draw your own labyrinth and then color it. You can do your own design or copy one of the designs that you found particularly meaningful.

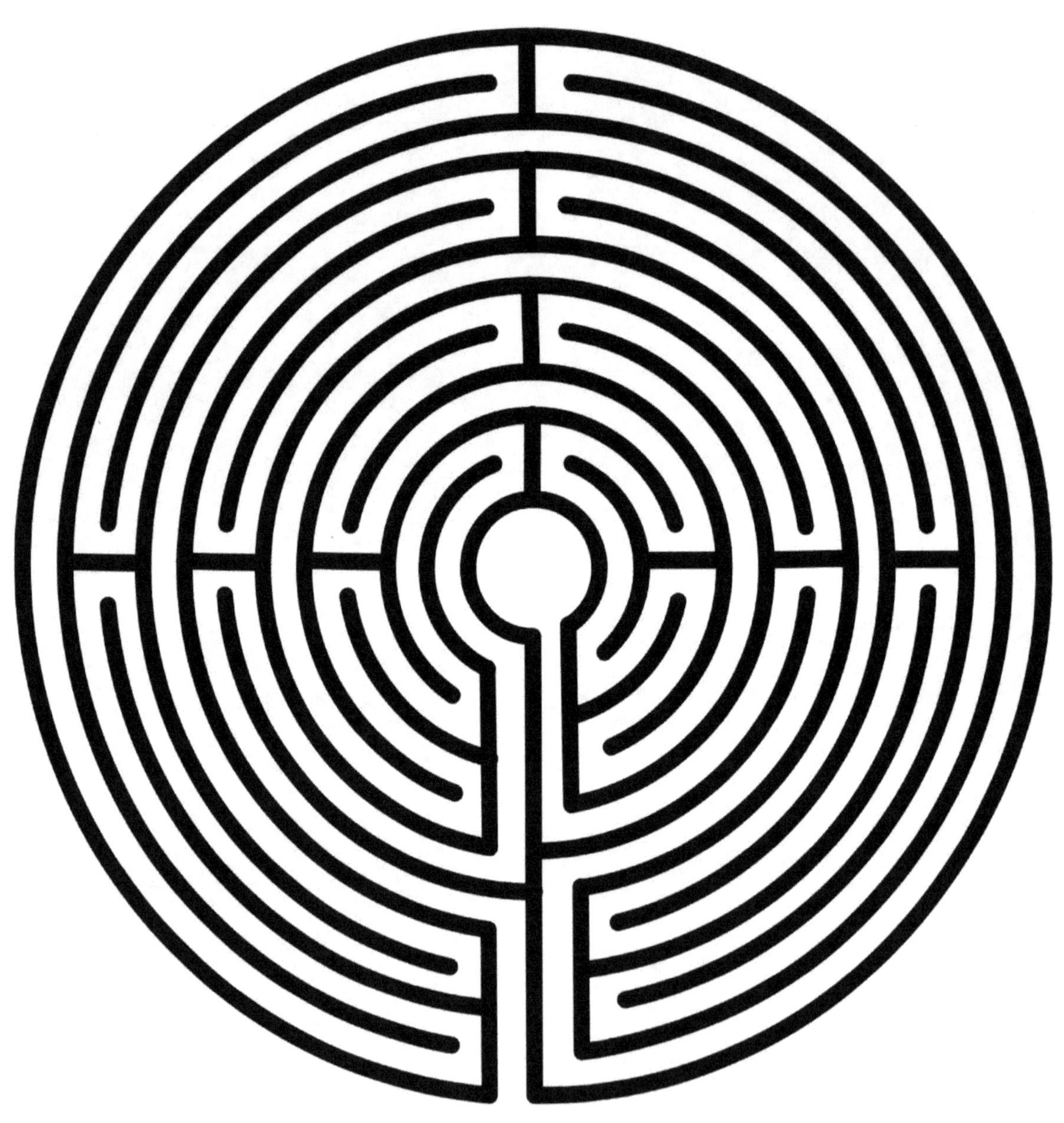

REFLECTIONS ON THIS BLOCK

Having walked the labyrinths in this block, what have you learned about your walk of faith? your relationship with God? ways in which you have difficulty being with the journey? parts of you that you hold back from fully engaging? lessons you are learning? Use this space to record your reflections on your journeys or arising from your journeys.

FINAL REFLECTIONS

Having walked all of these labyrinths in this book, review the journeys you have had. Look back on the reflections you wrote down at the end of each block. You have now really made these mini-pilgrimages part of your spiritual practice. What insights do you have overall from this? What has worked well for you on your journeys? How could this be helpful to your ongoing spiritual practice?

ABOUT THE AUTHOR

Christopher L. Smith has been involved in a diverse range of areas in terms of his training and experience. However, his approach through life is not to treat these as distinct dimensions, rather to see the connections across various aspects. This book is a good example of that. While studying at Yale Divinity School, he became aware of connections between his training in mathematics (including advanced work in computational geometry) and theological issues, particularly as seen in art and architecture. This background in sacred geometry prompts a different looking at labyrinths that allows him to guide the spiritual development and practice of others.He is grateful that he has been guided in his spiritual practices by people out of many different traditions including Methodist, Catholic (especially Franciscan and Jesuit), Charismatic, Episcopalian and his own Presbyterian.

At the time of preparing this book, Christopher's primary professional work was in the incorporation of spirituality into the therapeutic practice. In so doing, he has walked with people in their spiritual growth in ways that are in addition to his work as a minister and chaplain.

In addition to other books in this Sacred Colors series, Christopher has written on other topics. If you are interested in learning more about his writings, please look him up at http://AnAuthor.com/Christopher.

www.ingramcontent.com/pod-product-compliance
Lightning Source LLC
La Vergne TN
LVHW081321110826
845149LV00006B/1560

9780998529516